When
Words
Fail

Also by Debby Bellingham:

The Mentored Life - learning to live and love like Jesus (Bible Study)
The Mentored Life - learning to live and love like Jesus (Devotional)
The Long Shadow - a Lenten Journey in the Shadow of the Cross

With Dick Wiedehfeft:

Guidebook for Personal Devotions

When *Words* Fail

Prayers for prayers who can't find the words to pray

DEBBY BELLINGHAM

WESTBOW
PRESS®
A DIVISION OF THOMAS NELSON
& ZONDERVAN

WestBow Press books may be ordered through booksellers or by contacting:

WestBow Press
A Division of Thomas Nelson & Zondervan
1663 Liberty Drive
Bloomington, IN 47403
www.westbowpress.com
844-714-3454

ISBN: 978-1-6642-8023-6 (sc)
ISBN: 978-1-6642-8022-9 (e)

Print information available on the last page.

WestBow Press rev. date: 10/27/2022

This book is dedicated to the breath of God and those
through whom God's breath reaches me:
my husband, Jack, and my love hive (you know who you are).

God is as near as your breath. To pray, just inhale. D.B.

Acknowledgments

I would not be who I am without the love and support of my husband, Jack. He contains my whole person: body, soul, mind, and spirit and provides space for me to become who God created me to be. I love him forever.

Thank you to Ashley Fraser, Noelle L'Etoile, Georgia Price, and Esther Sprague—a team who out of love for God and me called many strategic, prayer, and encouragement meetings. They kept me on target and used their wisdom and gifts to make this book a reality.

My deep gratitude rests with the 48 readers who vetted my 1200+ prayers and culled the number down to 365. I asked them to read the prayers with their hearts, to ask the Holy Spirit to indicate which prayers were useful for the purposes of God. Their hard and faithful work is what I offer to you now.

Amy Mays
Andrea McGovern
Andrei Goga
Ashley Frazer
Aubrey Philbrick
Becki Low
Cher Coniglio
Cindy Steele
Deborah Suess
Denise Follina
Esther Sprague
Gay Jeffery
Georgene Usher
Georgia Price

Heidi Haring
Jack Bellingham
Janie Merkle
Jen Glenn
Joyce Dreier
Joyce Gartrell
Joyce Young
Julia Cho
Kate McNabb
Kate Peper
Kim Cruz
Kristi Kincheloe
Kristin Jones
Lisa Litsey

LIz Coniglio   Robert Glenn
Marcy Wigeri van Edema   Sharon Demko
Maria Maldonado   Sharon Vigilante
Marlene Hekkert   Sheila Dunning
Martha Jacobson   Sherilyn Stolz
Mary Anne McKenna   Tamaki Layman
Melissa Markus   Tassy Menudier
Noelle L'Etoile   Tom Giles
Nora Bertacchi   Virginia Kirkland
Pat Houk   Wendy Wallin

I'm always grateful to the people who subscribe to my (almost) daily prayer. They regularly visit my heart's prayer. Their support of my life's needs and their words of encouragement bless me immensely.

And believe it or not, I'd like to thank the occurrence of cancer for spurring me on to great love and good works. When I was first diagnosed with it in 2001, my spiritual director at that time told me cancer would become one of my best spiritual guides. She was right. Shortly after this diagnosis, I had a powerful time of prayer. Here is the gist of the prayer time:

I was scheduled to leave for a personal prayer retreat several days after I received the diagnosis. I trusted that God knew the timing of the diagnosis and the retreat, so I went ahead with my plans. During the first day of my time away, the Lord gave me a wonderful prayer experience. Often, I use my imagination when I pray, putting myself in the scene I'm reading, letting myself become one of the people with whom Jesus interacts. This is a very powerful and evocative means of praying. On this day, I was praying with the events of the last supper from Mark 14.

When the disciples and I got to the upper room, Jesus was there waiting for us. He opened the door to us and invited me alone to join him, leaving the other disciples outside the door. He and I were having a wonderful, intimate meal together, really enjoying each other's company. I'm sure you know the feeling, the pleasure you have when you're sharing dinner with someone you really care about, the atmosphere of closeness and fun, the warmth of the conversation. This was what I was feeling as Jesus and I sat across the table from one another.

In the midst of our meal, Jesus said to me, "Debby, there is a betrayer in our midst."

"Yes, Lord, I know. It is this cancer that is growing in me."

Pause

"This betrayer is the opposite of me," Jesus said.

"I know, Lord."

"This betrayer breeds death," he added.

During this dialogue, the presence of the betrayer began to become substantive, real, taking a form. I felt the pressure of its nearness. Jesus invited me to turn around, look at it and tell him what I saw. I resisted, and Jesus patiently encouraged me to do so. It took a long time, but finally, I obeyed. I turned and behind me was a large red mass, surprisingly, not an ugly thing. Jesus told me I needed to sit with this betrayer for a time. I began to cry.

Jesus asked if I had anything to say to this betrayer.

The words that came out of my mouth surprised me, "Hello, friend."

I was shocked by this response.

"Why do you see this betrayer of your life as a friend?" he asked.

I responded, "Because it will serve me by bringing me closer to you. Anything that moves me closer to you I have to call my friend."

Jesus smiled and looked deep into my eyes. He gave me a piece of bread dipped in wine and said, "This bread and wine are my body and blood, broken and spilled for you. My body will carry yours. Every time you eat bread (any bread) and drink wine (any wine), remember I died for you and to carry this betrayer away."

At the end of this prayer time, I knew complete peace. I knew the worst that cancer could do to me was kill me, and then I'd be in the unmitigated presence of Jesus. So cancer and death held no fear for me. I could rest in the peace that passes all understanding.

And, of course, to God be the Glory. Thank you and amen.

With you on the journey,
Debby

Introduction

For years now, I have been waking every morning (well, most mornings) eager to hear God's voice of love. I get up, get my coffee, settle down in my prayer chair, and wait.

Sometimes, I hear God's voice in the Psalm I read or the hymn that runs through my mind. Sometimes I see God's love in the beauty or the loneliness outside my window here in the Hudson Valley of New York. There are mornings my dogs tell me of God's great love through their affection and demands. Occasionally, a photograph or painting stirs my heart to recognize God's love in a profound or simple way. Sometimes, all is quiet, and my faith must trust God's love is actively pursuing me even when my soul is still.

Some mornings, my heart is numb, dulled by anxiety or pain, and there are no words in my soul to give voice to the contents of my heart. Other times, I'm lost in awe and wonder, and my heart can't capture adequate words to express my delight.

You will occasionally read words from God's heart spoken directly to my heart. These are the impressions the Spirit gave me during our time of communion. They are in quotes because I heard them as God's voice of love to me. They are not intended to be God's word for all human-kind. But maybe you will hear God's whisper in God's messages to me.

The prayers in this book are the fruit of years of such mornings. And it is my prayer that they will guide you into deeper communion with the God who loves you and that they will give voice to your heart's prayer when your words fail.

Read them a day at a time, meditate on them, and carry them with you through your day. Or use the index to find a prayer that matches your heart's tenor. Make these prayers yours as they rise like incense before the throne of God. They are yours—a gift God has given me, which I freely and joyfully give to you.

With you on the journey,
Debby Bellingham

1.

Wake up, oh my soul, shake off sleep, pay attention to the day, the birds, the sun, the warmth! Be gone, all things which make me fearful and numb, may my mind be free of thoughts that cause a shadow on the bright morning of this new day. Wake up, put on joy and courage! There is a great race to run today. True, it is the narrow road, not the easy road, and apart from God's feeding of my soul, God's strengthening my gait, I would tire and lay down in defeat. Oh God, no source of energy or sustenance can be your equal. Your power is ever new, ever young, and endures through all days and years. You are the eternal, abundant flow of fresh water on which my soul depends. When I trust in my power, I fade, I droop, and I die. I draw my strength for the day from you; I lean upon you; you are my stronghold, the one who shows me love. Thank you and amen.

2.

Oh, loving and welcoming Father, this day, your door is open, and you wait to receive me. My sin you've pardoned, the errors of my sin-bent ways you've forgotten. You are just glad to have me home. As I enter your presence, you offer joy to refresh me, and you guide me to the beautiful accommodations prepared for me, including a luxurious robe! When I attempt to refuse your provision because I feel I don't deserve your attention, you embrace me with your mercy, saying to me, "My door is always open; you are always welcome." Oh Lord, what would I do without you? You who lead me home. When I feel more despair than joy, I will run into your arms. I believe your invitation, I am welcomed home. Thank you and amen.

3.

Oh my Savior, the one who heals, I come before you to pray for health for myself and my friends. I am confident that your unending love will bring wholeness and restoration to our broken bodies and souls. Yet, as much as our bodies long to be relieved of the pain or inconvenience of illness, our hearts know our true need: to be healed in our soul, done with ailments of the spirit. We are well aware of what we want; we are not so in tune with what we need! You've planted in us seeds of truth. Let them sprout and grow and take over the space where unconscious pride has taken root. These seeds of truth bear the fruit of healing. Come great gardener, tend your garden. Thank you and amen.

4.

From the morning's first light until the stars gentle shimmer and the moon's glow are seen, three things rush to fill the space and time: faith (trust in God's presence), hope (an assurance of God's benevolence), and love (a giving and receiving of God's self). These three will outlast the earth and the heavens. Thank you and amen.

5.

Faith in Christ is what keeps my spirits lifted when the road toward home is steep and seems to never end. Hope in Christ is what guides my steps toward heaven's gates. And beyond these, love for Christ possesses my heart and motivates me to keep moving. I am headed home. I will see Christ, who loved me first and gave himself for me. We shall tenderly touch each other's face. Tears of joy will wet our cheeks; smiles, hugs, and dancing shall commence. This hope fuels my steps. Thank you, Jesus, and amen.

6.

~~~~~~~

Today, right now, always, the gate to your presence is open wide. I enter and you welcome me with a Father's love. I stand still in that embrace, letting myself relax and lean into your chest. You whisper that my sins are pardoned, my past wrongs are forgotten. "Well done," you tell me, and it is true. My future is secure. I am still. I need this respite of mercy, this reminder that you are my home, you are my guide especially when indifference rather than joy feels like my home base. Your gate is open, your ear is ready to hear my prayer, your joy is given. I stand still in your embrace. Thank you and amen.

7.

~~~~~~~

Today, my God, I love only your good pleasure for me, not my own. I desire nothing of you, except what your goodness wills for me. No love the world offers can compare with yours. You are full of tenderness and caring. You ignite my soul with the sweetness of belonging to you. You are full of holy affection, and you perfect my love. My many desires bring me to you. When united with your will I find the crosses I must bear easy, and death holds no fear. Today, I give my heart to you alone. Your love is enough. Thank you and amen.

8.

~~~~~~~

You are the author of faith, the word that is eternal, your Spirit keeps the flame of faith alive; Faith, like you, is always the same, always moving toward completion. Humbly, we long for you and humbly ask for our faith to increase, accomplishing its work. By faith's light we see reality, the clouds of doubt, the shadow of fear must disperse and we see you. Thank you and amen.

9.

Christ, come walk alongside me, go ahead of me this day, follow me with your mercy, be the ruler of my life. Christ, grow large within me, be the ground on which I stand, be the hope of my future, never leave me. Christ, be the power of all the work I do today, be the joy of all my leisure, surround me with your song, protect me against harm. Christ, grant me peace as I rest, wisdom as I converse, energy for my life, be the light of my life. Thank you and amen.

10.

It is possible, by God's grace, to live my life ready to bring relief and help to my fellow saints; to prefer following Jesus over the world's wealth and people's honor; to contently take my place in God's plan for the kingdom; to understand (at least to glimpse) the sacred mysteries. Oh, Lord Jesus, my leader, and my power bring me to safety, teach me what you need me to know, increase your light within me. Thank you and amen.

11.

Loving Father, I have run away from home, snuck out at night so as not to face you. I admit my foolishness, the way I've wasted the kindness you offer. I fear I am far from home, outside the reach of your grace. A whisper reaches my ear, your voice calling my name. I rise above my fear of banishment and the shame of my own ignorance; I recognize the wrong I've done, the harm I've caused, and dare to return to you, Lord. Your voice calling my name gives me courage and hope; I'm wanted still. I approach home clothed with disapproval, your approach shocks me. My dirty face, foul stench, and tattered garments do not stop your embrace. You sweep me up into your arms as if I were a child, your tears of joy clean my face. I am home. Lord, my Father at all times, whether I am foolishly away from home, or contently restored in your embrace, grant me the grace to cease my wandering; bind my heart to your compassionate, forgiving, and ever-caring heart. Embrace me with your pardon and peace. Thank you and amen.

12.

Now is the best time to come home, your open gate invites me to enter. I look within and see You, arms spread, a smile on your face ready to receive me into your embrace. You lift me to your chest and swing me around in a circle of joy. I am confident of my acceptance, no sin clings to me, no past haunts me, I am your beloved child home at last. Oh mercy that holds me close, Oh door that is always open, I depend upon your faithfulness and constancy to bring me home. When joy seems flat and despair rising, I recall your fatherly face, your open door, and your listening ear and I have the power to stand against the rising discouragement and choose delight. Thank you and amen.

13.

Wake up. Take courage. It is a new day, a new race to run. Leave behind fear and anxiety. It's true the road ahead is not easy: promises to keep, chores to accomplish, health challenges to face; but the mighty God, tireless and creative, is the source of your energy and your inspiration. From day to day and year to year, he strengthens you. From his plenty, he supplies you with refreshment and sustenance for the day to come. Trust in him. You know when you rely on your own resources you run out of energy and determination, your dreams fade and you lose sight of your goal. Trust in him and run! Thank you and amen.

14.

The sky cannot be doubted: it speaks your praise aloud with unique colors and the promise of needed rain. The thirsty earth cries for relief. You will supply all that is needed. Let me always look up to remember your greatness and your faithfulness. Thank you and amen.

15.

Settle down, my soul, the Lord is near you. Trust God as you carry the sorrow and the pain your circumstance requires. God cares for your life, every aspect of it. He remains faithful through all the ups and downs, the ins and outs. So settle down, your best friend, your shepherd Jesus remains near and guides you to a place of rest and blessing. Settle down, my soul, God will prove himself as faithful in the future as he has been in the past. He has promised a bright arrival to your forever home; don't worry, maintain your hope, even though the winds blow and the waves rise, his voice still rules their patterns. You can trust his care. Thank you and amen.

16.

Heaven is filled with saints who passed through suffering and entered your realm of light. Their spirits are bright with glory, they sit with you on thrones in the eternal day of your sunlight. One day, I'll join them, I will no longer know hunger or thirst; I'm on my way now. Come Holy Spirit, prepare me today for heaven. Thank you and amen.

17.

To you belong the glory, Jesus. You conquered death when you rose from its hold. You've won an endless victory. The grave proved empty when the angels rolled away the stone, even your grave clothes were left behind. Nothing of death was carried forward. You lovingly greet me this morning; your victory over death forces death to depart, taking with it all my fear and sadness. Gladness and triumph abide and I sing thanks to the living Christ. In such moments, no doubt remains; I know life without you is empty and with you is full. I walk confidently into the day, your power will bring me to the end of it and you will get all my glory. Thank you and amen.

18.

Jesus, you are the best of friends, always available and always kind. I feel the healing of my wounded soul in your presence; focusing on you settles my scurrying mind. You gather the scattered parts of my heart, bringing me to a still place; my breathing quiets, my heart beats in rhythm with yours. I am perfectly safe. No hunger, no thirst for you have supplied all I need. The load of my life feels less burdensome when I remember you accompany me, speaking the exact encouragement I need to hear: I am capable, I am entrusted, I am broken and beloved, I am valuable. Jesus, you are the best of friends, constantly loving, I look forward to the day when your kindness will be perfected and I will see you face to face. Thank you and amen.

19.

I bless you, Creator, your first act in the creation account was to call forth light from the darkness. Do it again, I beg; let there be light in this dark and chaotic world and in my shadowy heart. In the light of day I can more easily cling to your wisdom, in the dark of night I can be overcome with doubts. Hear my prayer, to remember in the night what you've shown me in the day. Otherwise, I lose sight of my eternal goal and get lost in life's temporal demands. Hang on to me this day, let me set aside the sin that clings and ignore the taunts of my errored past. I follow you through the gates of heaven. Thank you and amen.

20.

Lord, you have said there is forgiveness for those who admit their sin and their desire to change; so properly ashamed, and aptly confident in your word, I come. I have sinned, Lord, I have turned away from your love. Forgive me, heal me, set me on your path. It's easy to lose my way, stumble into darkness, God, I count on your ear that listens beyond my thoughtless actions. I depend upon your goodness to show me mercy when I offend you and I will continue to do so until the day I die. This is who you are. Thank you and amen.

21.

God's love, more excellent than any other, the bliss of eternity come to me, make your home within my heart, and let your faithful mercy mark me as your own. Jesus, founder of compassion, source of pure and complete love, visit me this morning with your saving power. My heart is weak and quaking; strengthen it with your presence, complete what you've begun in me. I pray each day to be more and more transformed into your image. As I gaze at you, I am inclined toward purity and holiness. I see your victorious glory, and I exchange my brokenness for your wholeness. It is easy to hold this truth in the quiet of the morning, but Lord, remind me through the day to let the wonder of your love move me to praise and obedience. Thank you and amen.

22.

Darkness is settling over the earth, daylight has faded, and I call to you, my Father. You rule over the night and the morning; your light never fades. Shine within my soul, within my home. Nothing about my day and my heart's actions are unknown to you. I give you all the fruits and failures of this day. I ask that as I rest, your love will possess my heart. Thank you and amen.

23.

Oh my soul, call on God, the one who saves you. Rest now in the shade of his protection. Return to the quiet place, the place where dismay is banished. God keeps you; no hostile enemy may trespass. The wildness and chaos of the day must remain outside this hidden place, this quiet place. Begin again, set your heart on loving God; He will clothe you in protective gear. Resolve to call on him when trouble bothers you so that God can quickly save you. There will be grief to bear; he will reward you for bearing it with hope. Hold tight. Begin again. Thank you and amen.

24.

Like a fire burned down, the day and my heart reignite with the rising sun. The darkness that blinded me must depart. Lord, Jesus, Son of the Morning, you have given me a new beginning as this new day begins. I pledge to hold to truth spoken and received, to acts motivated by love, not self-interest, to treat my body with the respect it deserves. Lord of all, you know the path ahead of me, and by the end of the day, it will be no surprise to you how I have walked it. Let me live it in a way that brings you glory, praise, and honor. In the name of the Father, the Son, and the Holy Spirit. Thank you and amen.

25.

In the quiet of this morning, as I am still, I feel the weight of my guilt, the subtle ways I have violated love. I am keenly aware of my shortcomings and the gap between the wholeness I desire and the brokenness of my experience. Conflict surrounds me, condemning fear whispers within me. Who can help me? To whom can I turn? God of grace, you alone are the source of hope. You welcome my broken self and my heart that knows its lack. My scattered parts need unity, and my confused self needs clarity. Please grant what is needed: a deep, interior alignment with truth. From this centered, solid self, the fruit of love can blossom. Humility will spread a carpet of welcome. Sorrow over slip-ups will correct me. My deep desire to know you and live for you will increase its authority. All you ask is that I place my trust in your saving work and put all my eggs in the basket of Christ's great love. Thank you and amen.

26.

Lord, you are the reason I slept safely through the night and woke refreshed and ready for this new day. (One day, I'll wake into the eternal day, and all will be light.) With the rising sun, I rise to do my best to live only for your glory. Help me by melting away my enemies, within and without, with your light and warmth. Fill me with your Spirit and guard my mind and my heart, so my deeds prove your love. Thank you and amen.

27.

Grant me the grace, oh Lord of hopefulness and joy, to trust you with the day you've set before me. Let nothing shatter the bliss you share with me as we sit together this morning. As the day unfolds, and the work you've given requires my attention, let your strength and your spirit of readiness be what energizes me. As the day closes, with my labors concluded, let me remember the ways you will have been faithful to me throughout the hours of this day, and may I rest in your peace. Thank you and amen.

28.

Lord, do unto me as you've done unto saints before me; let your wondrous works of grace flow through me. Your kind love has chosen me; you've given me particular gifts to offer that will bring your loved ones closer to your heart. I give you the glory. May your spirit, invested in me, increase my stake of heavenly riches for the benefit of the ones who you will feed through me. Lord, keep your eyes on me. Grant me grace to follow you into the joy of eternity that begins now. Thank you and amen.

29.

There is something sacred and holy about a building dedicated to you: shrines, cathedrals, temples, even simple churches are created to draw me into your presence, to remind me of your power, and to bring you glory. Christ, you are the foundation of all these edifices, the reason they exist. Bind the people who worship within them together. Be our head, our starting place, our sure hope. Thank you and amen.

30.

To not hurl hurtful words, to not return nastiness, to walk toward the one with whom I disagree, to listen more than I speak: these are the signs of love, the evidence of your presence, the way of the cross that Christ invites me to embrace. Few are the extreme sufferings that will be mine to bear, but plenty are the daily dyings that pave the way toward your Kingdom. Each day brings the opportunity to say no to my false self, with its ego-driven opinions and positions, and yes to your gift of life. Dear Jesus, grant me the grace to look through the choices set before me into your loving, death-defeating face and to follow you through death into life. Thank you and amen.

31.

Lord, all my praise and worship is only a drop in the bucket of the debt I owe you. Your love, so amazing, cannot be repaid. I can only receive it and wonder at the daily grace you give me—blessings uncountable, mercies that stretch from dawn to dawn. This morning, I ready my heart to hear your word. Hear mine: I love you. In response to your kindness, I serve you and your creation. I know not what today holds, but I know I will find you hidden throughout its minutes. I will bless you and live in awe of your beautiful ways. Thank you and amen.

32.

God, you are the still point from which all creation gains its energy. I am still with you now to enable me to be about the work of the day guided by your power. This day, lived faithfully, prepares me for the eternal day, the day where you are my sun, and I completely reflect your glory. Thank you and amen.

33.

Victor of the conflict, take your seat, the seat of glory, the throne of your kingdom. You're the triumph. Even death must bow to you. You emerged victorious, rescuer of the world, King of life who lives forever. I wake to a snow-covered world this morning with gladness in my soul! The gates of heaven open, and Jesus welcomes me into his joy. You emerged victorious, rescuer of the world, King of Life who lives forever. Lord, you took on the fight against sin and death, and it appeared they won. But your life proved impossible to kill. You prevailed over death and sin, made heaven accessible and hell not mine. You emerged victorious, rescuer of the world, King of Life who lives forever. My victory, my rescuer, my King. Thank you and amen.

34.

All my heart praises you; my joy knows you are its source, my fear changes to trust when I pause and focus on your promise of provision; worry dissipates in the warmth of your sunrise. How does my discouragement praise you? I lay it before you, and it melts like the snow under the warm sun. You have always been there for me; you have saved me countless times from the enemy's clutches and my own folly. Thank you. I rejoice and let my heart rise in gladness as the sun rises this morning, showing the snow-dotted garden. Insecurity and doubt get turned away from my doorstep because you guard my home. I can see their emptiness and clumsiness as they depart from your presence. You alone are the one who announces the validity of my life, and you have called me valued. Thank you. Under your rule, prejudice and harmfulness are eliminated from my heart. There is nothing in me that seeks destruction and the promotion of my cause at the cost of others. You are worthy of determining the merit and the truth of my case. In you is relief from the pressure of my circumstance. My days are held in your heart. I know you. You will never abandon me. All my heart praises you. Thank you and amen. [A prayer based on Psalm 9]

35.

Rise up, rise up my soul, rise up to meet your God. The sunrise is amazingly beautiful, and God, you are more beautiful still. The pink and purple clouds, the diamonds glittering on the grass, the shimmer of the spider webs are shadows of your true loveliness. Thanks for the awe the beauty of the morning inspires. It turns my soul to you. And now, the brightness of the sun forces me to shade my eyes. Your glory is sun-like, unapproachable without a guard. Thank you and amen.

36.

Oh Christ, brilliant one and joyful light, out of your delight, the stars were born. Wonder of wonders! Eternal word joined flesh as your yes met Mary's, and you settled in her womb. Oh, loving Father, your generosity far exceeds my meager hopes. Your compassion outruns me and prevents my falling, falling, falling onto the rocks of hell. You entered Mary's womb with a donor card, ready to give your life so your heart could become mine. The darkness of night seemed to own our war-torn world when you quietly set up your camp amid the strife. Your intention, to win the prize of the world you created. You are the firstborn, the new adam; you are the spouse of your bride, the church; you are the shining sun that chases away the darkness. You have won your prize! I now answer to the name beloved. Perfect, I am not, but I trust in your pity. Thank you and amen.

37.

Lord, despair knocks on the door. I arm myself with remembering your call to me and your cross-proved mercy toward me. I pause before I answer the knock and attend to the spark of holy love you've placed within me. Selah. Courage to turn away despair arises when I remember who you are: God of glory, Son of humility, Spirit of hope. Praising you energizes me. I can open the door. Despair, like a doormat, serves to ready me for your presence. Thank you and amen.

38.

Thy Kingdom come. Your kingdom comes with such rich blessings, sustenance, and delight. I know it in glimpses now, but try to live in its fuller revelation day by day. When I let myself wander from your city, oh Lord, my heart and my words are heavy, but when I contemplate your promises, the joy, the glory, the bliss beyond compare, my heart is buoyed and light. In the quiet of this morning, before I wander off into the duties and joys this day holds in store, I contemplate your kingdom. Such activity provides solace for my sorrows, healing for my wounds. Love increases in my heart, life seems grand, and I experience your peace and calm. Like you, Jesus, with my eyes fixed on the joy set before me, I resolve to enter your kingdom. I will cooperate with the glory of grace. I will make room in my mind for light. I will grasp the fullness of your kingdom with my hope until hope is no longer needed because I see you face to face. In the meantime, I know you are on my side. I belong to you; now, with my eager faith and forever, transformed by your glory. Thank you and amen.

39.

Listen! You can hear his approach. Our Savior comes near! Oh heart of mine, prepare a throne and sing his praise. He comes and releases my imprisoned will; Satan's hold is broken, and I move about unfettered. He comes and seals the gaps in my broken heart; I am filled with the wine of his mercy and pour it out to those I meet. He comes and enriches my poor soul; I am content with the bounty of his presence. Let's sing together of his Kingdom come. We welcome you, loving Jesus. Come rule our hearts with your peace. Thank you and amen.

40.

Holy Father, I was not there to look into the infant Jesus' eyes, nor see the wonder on the face of Joseph as he laid him in the manger; I did not watch Mary tenderly hold him close against the cold. But I meet him daily in mysterious guises. I behold his face in the scriptures. I care for him in my neighbor. I am awed by him in the Eucharist. I embrace him to my heart and know that he is mine. Thank you and amen.

41.

I rise in the darkness and pray your wisdom will shine upon me as I pray; as the sky lightens, may I hear and heed the Spirit's voice. Oh, living Word, grant me wisdom to discern the way of your Kingdom this day. Stir up faith, diminish doubt, cast out fear and distrust. Your light has dawned upon my heart, and only peace remains. I will follow as you lead. Thank you and amen.

42.

Lord, grant me the grace to enter this new day with your love as the source of all my work, all my thoughts, words, and actions. You've assigned me a particular task to accomplish. I receive it with joy, for I know I will meet you in the doing of it, and good will be the outcome. Yoked with you, the work will be easy to bear, and you will be able to hear even my whispers. The work we do prepares me for heaven, so I take it up joyfully. I trust your good will and walk through this day and its labors with you at my side. Thank you and amen.

43.

I am not the trailblazer. Almighty Father, you have gone out into my day, preparing it for me. As I follow you, I walk into places of grace and mercy, places of power and eloquence. Thank you, God. I can walk with humble confidence, and the stage is set for your Spirit to minister. Jesus, you are the one who leads. From your obedience, I learn obedience and enter your joy. Come Holy Spirit. Thank you and amen.

44.

Oh God, it is for you my soul thirsts, come down and moisten my dry heart. Gideon laid his fleece, and you showered it with dew and refreshed the city with rain. The sun rises, bringing light upon this dark earth; shower, refresh, and rise upon me, oh Lord. I do not hope in vain. You will show me yourself. Come Holy Spirit. Thank you and amen.

45.

My desire to know and serve you is aided when I remember how you have been faithful to all the saints before me who have sought you. I read of hope in you that was not disappointed—how abundant blessings flowed from your hand! I read of how your presence and truth sustained the trusting one—how you graciously pardon those who seek you. I need this same you today. Nothing can stand against me. Jesus Christ is on my side—no sore throat, no nagging self-doubts, no lack of energy can separate me from the love Jesus has for me. He didn't let death keep him from me. He won't let life keep me from him. Thank you and amen.

46.

I trust in your kindness, Lord, as I come before you weighed by guilt and asking for mercy. My sin dirties me; wash me clean. The actions of my sins have harmed others, including me, but truly it is against you I have sinned. I enter the shower of your kindness, and my sin gets carried away down the drain. Create a new heart within me, one that is clean and beats with your mercy. Remake my mind so that it thinks as you do. Grant me the grace of your favor. I tire and faint without the sustenance of your support. Thank you and amen.

47.

Lord, I remember the saints who have gone before me and left a legacy for me to follow, and like them, may my life overflow with kind deeds provoked by love. Let me be generous because you are so giving, let me offer solace because I have been so comforted, let me stand strong in the face of blind injustice and act with kindness toward all my neighbors. I long for a clean heart, to be a lamp that shines your light, to rely on you for strength, and to possess a humility that lets others come to my aid. Thank you and amen.

48.

Oh Lord, God, you keep faith forever. Faith is the assurance of things hoped for, the conviction of things not seen. You keep faith in me; you are convinced that your good work in me will come to its perfection. You believe in me. I cannot see the wholeness you are creating in me, but you do. You keep faith that all will be as you envision it; you see the me you intended me to be and know I will emerge. You keep faith, hold steady, remain fixed on the target: me, complete and whole. You never tire of working to lift me from shame, nourish my soul and my body, release me to walk about freely, open my eyes to the minute and grand beauty. You keep faith for me; you love the ways I line up with your goodness. You teach me to value what you value. Caring for the least of these; you strengthen me to stand against what operates against your love. You reign forever and keep faith forever. Praise you, God. Thank you and amen. [A prayer based on Psalm 146:5-10]

49.

Jesus is ready to listen to all my complaints and burdens. He's such a good friend. I am so blessed to be able to call upon him any time. Why do I forget to take advantage of such a source of respite and comfort? I carry the pain on my own, forgetting to talk with Jesus about it. Though there is conflict all around me, I am not discouraged. I can talk to the Prince of Peace, who knows me and how I am impacted by it. When I feel burdened and laden with sorrow, there is one place I can go to find solace—to Jesus, my precious Savior. Friends are not always available. Jesus is. Thank you for your sheltering arms and power to protect. Thank you and amen.

50.

There are moments when I recognize how short life is, how quickly it passes. In these moments, Lord, stay near me. No one can afford me the help and comfort I need better than you. Stay near. There are moments when I look around and see only the evolving decay of the world. Changeless Lord, stay near me. There are moments when the tempter's power is strong, and your grace alone strengthens me to choose life. I need you to be my guide in times of darkness and in times of light. Lord, stay near. Even though life has sorrow and tears, your blessing carries me through. Even death has no sting when you are near me. In the end, when my time draws close, your word will have proven true: heaven dawns, shadows flee, in life and death, Lord, stay near me. Thank you and amen.

51.

I invite all of God's creation to join with me in praising our Lord and King. Moon and stars that illuminate the night, sun that heralds the new day: join me in a fresh beginning. Let's praise him! Wind that blows where it will, snow that falls covering all in white: let's praise him. Rivers that flow, singing with your current to your Lord. Come earth, praise God with your fertile produce, the beauty of your flowers honor the Lord, and your fruit feeds God's creatures. And humankind, praise our God by having tender hearts, ready to forgive. Let us honor our God by casting on him our pain and sorrow. We all bless you, our Creator, and are humbled by your care for us. Thank you, Father, Son, and Holy Spirit. Alleluia. Thank you and amen.

52.

There is power in your name, Jesus. Let me honor and respect it as the angels do. I crown you with the beats of my heart. Its rhythms are all I have to offer. You have chosen and ransomed me. I praise you and acknowledge your rule over my life. Let all the earth and all people honor you. I join the song that never ends, sung by saints throughout eternity, praising you and naming you King. Thank you and amen.

53.

Oh Lord, I am so grateful for the union I share with other believers. Your Spirit binds us together, and the sweetness of our fellowship is a taste of heaven. I count on my friends to carry my needs to you, as I carry theirs. We are joined in our sorrows and our joys. Even though miles and even death separate us, as sad as this might be, our hearts remain connected, confident we will meet again. And one day, we will meet in eternity, done with sin and alive to love. Thank you and amen.

54.

Dear Lord, just as you broke the loaves beside the sea of Galilee, feeding the crowds, would you break open the bread of your word and feed me this morning? I seek you beyond the pages of scripture. Your words are the door I walk through to meet you. I am waiting for your presence. Break the chains that keep me captive, the habits that bind me to death so that peace, not frantic hoarding, rules my days. You are the food of my life. Your word rescues me. Your love teaches me to love. Send your Spirit today to open my eyes to see your face through the scriptures, through my writings, through my encounters. Come, walk with me. Thank you and amen.

55.

I breathe air saturated with your life. You are my breath; each inhalation brings me newness, another opportunity to love. Breathe deeply and remember the source. Purify my heart with the oxygen of your holiness; course through my veins until I am one with your will and am strengthened to act and suffer as you guide. I breathe until eternity, until perfection. Come Holy Spirit, breath of God, enter and sustain; flow out and cleanse. Thank you and amen.

56.

I love waking early and greeting the sun as it rises in all its splendor; you, though, Lord Jesus, are brighter and more beautiful than the morning star. You chase the dark away from my heart and grant me light to see the path of the day. Your humble birth masked your divinity, maker, ruler, and savior; wise ones brought you treasures of the earth, born out of their desire to honor you. More precious to you, though, is my heart offered to you, my prayers entrusted to you. These are what grant me your favor. Bright morning star, break upon every minute of my day. I need your aid to find my way to worship you in all I do. Thank you and amen.

57.

Oh heavenly Father, gather all your children into your arms, the only safe place to be held, the sweetest refuge to be found. Your love binds me to you, and nothing can separate us, not life nor death. Your grace abounds in the places where I sorrow and accompanies me through joys and grief. Your loving purpose is to bring me home, pure and holy. Come Holy Spirit. I cooperate with your grace. Thank you and amen.

58.

$\sim\sim\sim\sim\sim$

Good news: Jesus is alive! The cross is empty! Love, slain by death, yet lives! Praise you, Lord! Your resurrection allows you to save and heal here and now. Though your suffering continues in places where there is war, division, and brokenness, your love remains active even when hope has died. You call, and all people can respond. Your spirit leads them to you: the way, the truth, and the life. Your aliveness brings the good news and will continue to announce it until love reigns throughout the world. Thank you and amen.

59.

$\sim\sim\sim\sim\sim$

The transgressions I know about are always in my face, taunting me, shaming me, threatening to expose me as a fraud to the people around me. Still, the reality is that you are the one who matters in my world. My sin offends you, and it comes as no surprise to you. There is no denying I have failed, turned away from your path of life. I deserve your disapproval. Some of my favorite sins have been around for as long as I can remember. But I beg you, teach me wisdom from the inside out. I want my primary mode of operation to be truth. Lord, I tire of the long face attitude that sin leaves me with. Take me back to the place where my countenance lights with joy because of your mercy and love. I'll have something to say to my friends then, won't I? They'll want in on the connection with you! Lord, I need you to hold me back from shedding my sister's blood with my tongue, impatiently talking about her, demeaning her. Instead, let my tongue sing of your kindness and how great you are to save. Lord, my Lenten fast is offered out of love, not ritual nor expectation. You receive me with delight. Thank you and amen. [A prayer based on Psalm 51:3-6,12-14,17]

60.

Jesus Christ is the solid ground on which I stand. He is the beloved chosen savior, leader, and standard that holds all believers as one family—my one hope, and my constant help. Oh Lord, come here to this sacred parlor, tarry with me, show me your kindness as I share with you my heart's concerns. May I know your favor as I sit with you. Grant me my heart's desire and open my eyes to see its manifestation. Add to my life today what will remain with me in eternity. Prepare me to reign with you through time. Praise you, powerful and glorious Trinity, never beginning and never-ending. Thank you and amen.

61.

I love the Lord; let my heart express my joy. I join with saints living and alive forever coming before the throne because I am on my way to God's eternal and beautiful home. Those who don't know you will not sing, but I'm your child and cannot help but sing! Someday I'll know the sweetness of eternity, but even today, I nibble on appetizers, anticipating the feast. So let music sound, and tears be dried; I'm on my way to heaven! Thank you and amen.

62.

Oh God, is it true? Am I your city? Your word says you formed me to house your presence, and your word does not lie. Built upon the solid rock that never changes, I am perfectly safe and can rest secure. You satisfy me with the living water flowing from your heart of love. I have no want; your grace never fails. Your Spirit hovers within my spirit, sharing your power and glory, confirming your nearness, and guiding me as I pursue the life you've given. Through your mercy, I have all I want and need. The world's best will fade; the joy of knowing you will grow. Thank you and amen.

63.

Lord, you prepared an upper room and invited the loved ones to join you for the Passover meal. You still invite, and I still come; I come celebrating the offered Lamb and risen Lord. I receive the bread and the wine, and you take my sins and my sorrows. You wash my feet, serving and preparing me to serve. The joy and peace I have in you are endless; the love you give is beyond my comprehension. You have gone ahead and prepared a room for me, and you have returned to walk with me toward it. Thank you and amen.

64.

Oh, Jesus, you are such a friend. I come to you weighed down by all the wrongs I have done and all the wrongs that have been done to me, and you take them from me. I am so blessed to commune with you about all the details of my life. When I forget to talk with you, I feel restless, worried, and in pain. Lord, today I will encounter many temptations; I anticipate the enemy attempting to woo me into pretense, to hide me from genuine connections. Grant me security in you so I can be present to the people with whom I interact. Also, as I consider the trouble in my country and the world, I am tempted to react with anger or detachment. Lord, help me not add to the unrest but rather bring peace—your peace. I admit I am often afraid and know myself weak, but you know me intimately and do not despise me. You welcome me, hold me safe, and give me the courage to carry on. So I will. Thank you and amen.

65.

I wake each morning eager to hear your voice of love. I sit with you quietly, reading your word, praying, thinking of your ways. I take up my computer to capture our process. I do my part in writing your good news. But you are the one who enlivens the words I write. Your Spirit stirs my heart and gives me insights about which to write. I serve; you bless. You give what is needed to nourish my soul: cold dark seasons, warm pleasant ones. Your Spirit blows freshness; the sun shines light, and living water refreshes me. You are the maker of all things beautiful: the flowers outside my window, the stars that sprinkle the sky. All creation obeys your word; you tend your creation, birds and humans alike. Use me to tend your world. Thank you for all your provision. I give you back my heart. Thank you and amen.

66.

Lord, walking with you on the path your word illuminates brings confidence and joy to my heart. Doing your will creates more space in my life for you to dwell. Keep me mindful of the connection between trusting you and then doing what you ask. You know all the burdens and sorrows that are mine to carry. Trusting you, I carry them, fortified by your strength and favor. I lay down upon your altar, letting my false self receive the death-blow; I rise knowing your delight in me, your smile upon me, your joy lifting me. Like Mary, I sit at your feet; like the disciples, I walk where you lead. Grant me the grace to do what you say and go where you send. Replace my fear with trust. It is the only way to know peace and contentment. Thank you and amen.

67.

Today is your day, Lord. You own the hours and share them with me. Let me use them wisely, profitably for your design. I praise you, for you are my helper. I need not worry; you are always with me, granting me your aid. When I think about how kind you are, how you chose to offer salvation to me and all the world, my heart grows strong and cheerful. I enter this day, your day, covered in your protection; I know your joy and walk in peace. Thank you and amen.

68.

I live in this world created and owned by you, Father God, and when I listen, I hear the music of your composition. I take great comfort in remembering I belong to you, who lovingly created tulips, apple trees, and pugs. I look out my window and see the sweet peas climbing up the teepee I built for them. They move ever upward toward your sun. They call to me, "Come along, join our rising, stretch toward the light of the Son." All the beauty I behold originates in your lovely heart. You eagerly speak to me through your creation; the wind blows, and I know you are near. Sometimes I get discouraged when I think about the wrong in the world, the evil that seems so pervasive and dominant; Lord, let me remember that you are the ruler of this world. Evil is in its death throes. By your grace, I will live in your kingdom, glad that you reign. I will love as you have loved and overcome death in my little portion of this beautiful world you've created. Thank you and amen.

69.

To you belongs all glory, for you are the risen one, the one who conquered death, the Father's beloved son; death is forever defeated! The massive power of God rolled away the stone, and the detail-oriented power of God neatly folded the grave clothes. Jesus, you meet me this morning during our time of communion. In your presence, fear and worry evaporate. Gladness marks my heart, and I face the day with confidence because you lead me in your triumph. Forgive my forgetting to honor you, prince of life, for thinking I can manage on my own. Without you, life is void. Help me depend upon you, as I depend upon this chair to hold me. Your love never dies. It is my safeguard and my transport. Thank you and amen.

70.

The seas are wide; your mercy is wider. You come toward me with judgments in hand. I expect to hear accusations; instead, your words speak the truth. I am broken and beautiful. You feel my sorrows and understand my failings; your judgment is kind and leads me to freedom. Your love stretches beyond my imagination. Your heart always cares. Increase my faith to trust you more and live a life that reflects my gratitude for your goodness. Thank you and amen.

71.

Oh dear Lord, take my hand in yours. I depend upon you to lead me into the light. Strengthen me to firmly stand, though I am weary, needy, and feel alone. Through uncertainty, lead me to my sure home. When I am bored with the task I've been given, come near and brighten my outlook. When I dread doing the work before me, set your hand on mine, and let's do it together. Let the evening stars find me ready to rest, blessing you and content. Thank you and amen.

72.

O h, my soul, keep moving forward, eyes fixed on your crucified Jesus. Follow him even into battle against the enemy. He is the champion and has led the way through war into peace. His triumph causes Satan to flee. With my praise, hell shakes. United with all believers, I move toward God's kingdom. Let me be filled with hope, truth, and love. Christ, receive our songs of praise and glory. Thank you and amen.

73.

K ing David's birthplace was your own, and in it stood a manger where Mary laid you as you slept. Heaven's glory laid aside. You came to earth in humility and lived your holy life among the poor, the needy, and the disempowered. I imagine the trouble your holiness got you into as a child, the sorrow from which it saved you, and the grief to which it eventually led. One day I will see your holiness with my own eyes, for you promised that I shall also be where you are. Ah, redeeming love that transforms a manger into a throne, a holy life into a saving one, and a sinner into a star. Thank you and amen.

74.

John stands on the banks of the Jordan announcing your arrival. I heed his cry and look for your glad appearance. I make straight my inward paths so you can easily access my heart. Come, Jesus, be my Lord and Savior, my refuge and my reward. I need you as my flowers need the rain. Heal me from all ills—bodily, emotionally, and spiritually. Fill me and your world with love. You have won my freedom. I praise you, Jesus, along with the Father and the Holy Spirit. Thank you and amen.

75.

Oh precious head, who once knew glory and blessing, now hangs low because of sorrow and shame, wounded and mockingly crowned with thorns. I claim you as mine even in your suffering. For all you suffered was to benefit me. I was the condemned one. You were the one who paid the deadly penalty. The gap between what I deserve and what I receive humbles me. Look on me with favor and continue to save me by your grace. No words can adequately express my thanks for your gift of salvation. My only response is to ask you to make me yours and keep me loyal by your mercy. May my love for you ever increase. Thank you and amen.

76.

A prayer for marriages: Oh perfect love, beyond our comprehension, quietly I come before you asking for your blessing on my marriage, that our love will spring from your heart and never vary or weary. May we depend upon you as the source of our kindness and loyalty toward each other. Grant us the grace to always hold hope and humbly and bravely trust you in all that life presents. Give us joy even in times of sorrow, a peace that rules over strife, and a vision of a tomorrow where life and love will reach completion. Thank you and amen.

77.

If my heart were more aligned with God's, I would know calmness, peace, and light would illuminate the path leading to the lamb of God. I have experienced the blessedness of such closeness, and I long for it now. My soul needs refreshing, a new vision of the life of Jesus and a new immersion into his life-giving word. I remember the sweetness of the Spirit's ministry to my soul, the joy of spending time with the Lord. I am empty without such a connection. Lord, if there is some idol I cling to that is separating us, help me to let it go and smash it, leaving me free to worship you alone. Then, again, I will be close to you, calm and serene, and your light shall mark the path we walk toward home. Thank you and amen.

78.

O King of Glory, I worship you, I gratefully tell of your power that saves, your love that transforms; you are my defense and protection. I picture you young and old at the same time, joyfully receiving your children in a comfortable, royally appointed gazebo. I will speak of your might and grace. You are clothed in light as you parade through space. The clouds are your chariot, the storm your path. Your care is profound and bountiful: the air I breathe, the gift of vision, the beauty of the land and river. You sweetly offer me the necessities and joys of life. I depend upon you, for I am weak, and you constantly come through with tender mercy. You are patiently recreating me, aggressively defending me, gladly receiving me, and kindly befriending me. Your power is endless. Your love is changeless. The angels worship you, and so do I. For you have redeemed me, polished me, so my gifted glory shines through my brokenness. Praise you, Lord Jesus Christ, King of endless glory. Thank you and amen.

79.

Oh, Jesus, I pray that I will walk close to you, using the freedom you have given me to serve you and my neighbors. Whisper your kingdom secrets into my heart. I think they will cause me an air of sorrow and care. Help me bear them with grace and joy. Lord, I wake each morning eager to hear your voice of love and then to share it with the people you've given me to love. Let your winsome mercy be the tone of my words. Draw to yourself the ones who have lost sight of your goodness. Let me humbly leave a trail for them to follow that leads to your heart. Lord, let me never leave your side, teach me patience, let the work I do add sweetness and strength to my faith, may my trust in you triumph over the wrong I encounter within and without. I hope my life adds light to the world and that your peace marks my life. Thank you and amen.

80.

Oh, Jesus, I have promised to serve you with my life. Come close to me with your Lordship and your friendship. Grant me the courage to fight the malaise and guide me into energy and life. So many voices, so many choices—attune my ear to your particular accent. My fickle heart heeds the urgency of the instant. Please speak clearly and distinctly, instructing me so I walk in the path of the important. Thank you and amen.

81.

Today I will probably need to hear your reassurance: I belong to you. I will need your quickening: love the other now. And I will need your no: wait for life. Guard my soul and help me listen. Oh, Jesus, you have promised to bring me with you into your glory. Grant me the grace to follow you, Lord and friend. You have walked ahead, leaving footprints for me to follow. Be my strength as I try to step only where you have trod. Guide me, call me, draw me and receive me, Savior and friend. Thank you and amen.

82.

There are moments, Jesus, when my love for you is as complete as it can be. Now is one of them. You have given yourself to me, and for love of you, I let go of the foolish choices that cut me off from life. Your powerful grace saves. Thank you. Your love for me calls forth a loving response. I ponder the cost of your love, the cross, the crown of thorns, and gratitude bubbles up in my heart. In life and in death, my love will be yours. My very breath comes from your good hand, and with it, I will praise you. One day my earthly breath will be transformed into an eternal hum of praise, and at your feet, my love will be complete. Thank you and amen.

83.

We all have faith in something; mine is set on you, Lamb of God, who takes away the sins of the world (mine included). I will count on your grace for the strength to carry out my heart's desire, to live solely for you. You have died for me. I will live for you. Stir up a living fire that warms and purifies my love; may I remain faithful and true. As the day brings uncertainties about which path to tread, I will look to you to guide me into life. Choosing to remain close to you is comfort and joy. Death is ever knocking at my door. Remove its power over me. Instead, I open the door of my heart to trust and hope and welcome freedom into my life. Thank you and amen.

84.

Jesus, my savior, may your grace rest upon me. Father, my creator, may your endless love support me. Holy Spirit, my sustainer, may your favor supply me. May we be joined with one another and know joy beyond measure in this union. Thank you and amen.

85.

Lord, mark me with your blessing, fill my heart with joy and peace. Your love is mine; I can walk valiantly through the day as I follow your guidance and am protected by your power. May I faithfully hold to your truth and let the soil of my heart bear the fruits of your saving grace. I thank you for the joy of the good news. Thank you and amen.

86.

Lord, let be unto others as you have been to me. I hear your voice of love. Grant me the grace to be an echo, sounding your love to those around me. You've sought me, and I will seek the searching ones, the lonely ones. Lead me, Lord, to the living water, that I may help others find it and drink. Teach me the precious truth of your life and work, and grant my words the power to reach the secret places of many people's hearts. Lord, let my life overflow with the joy of your love. Use me, even me, as you will, where and when you will; let's go together into the world you love. Keep me faithful until faith is no longer needed, for I see you face to face. Thank you and amen.

87.

Lord Jesus, it gives me strength to know you think about me. Your thoughts are for my purity and freedom; and for my overcoming evil's influence in my mind, my body, and my heart; and for my walking along the road of truth that leads to life. You think about the joyous day when we will meet face to face. It brings such sweet comfort. Let it be. Thank you and amen.

88.

Truly, Lord, I lay aside my groans and mumbles and open my mind to the gladness of being known by you. I focus on your enduring mercy and your constant faithfulness to your creation. I appreciate the light you established that dispels the dark and the constant care you give us, satisfying our needs. I praise you for your kindness and the freshness your presence offers. Renew me this morning. Thank you and amen.

89.

Lord, lead me now in this day of action; in doing the work for which you've prepared me, I find my home. Your grace has made me strong. I am ready to stand firm against the advance of sin. Choosing life will give peace a chance to raise her voice, for she comes not by threats of war or armed military but by deeds of love and mercy. Lead your people, O valiant one; we follow with gladness; your presence is our hope and strength, your cross is our power and protection. We walk toward our heavenly home and the well done that awaits us. Thank you and amen.

90.

My only virtue is that you died for me. I have no holiness of my own, yet you invite me to come to you, so I do. I come. Desiring to be free of the constraints of death, I come to the lamb of God who takes away the sin of the world, mine included. My doubts and my troubled mind drive me to you, not away from you, for you are the source of peace. I come to you, the perfect host; your door is open to welcome me, a bath and a delicious meal await me. I can rest because your promises are true. I am invited to come to you, and I do. I come. Thank you and amen.

91.

Jesus, the joy of my heart, the wellspring of my life, and the light of the world, I heed your call. Nothing in the world satisfies completely; not this cup of coffee, not the morning sun on my face—unless they are received as gifts from your hand. Your truth is changeless, and your desire to save is constant. I seek you and discover your goodness. Ah, I'm content. I have eaten morsels of the living bread and long for the feast. I've sipped the living water and thirst for a full cup. Today, my restless heart will wander through valleys of peace, hills of impatience, and unknown landscapes. Cause me to pause during my day, feel your smile, and embrace my faith anew. Oh, Jesus, I want to stay close to you. Remove the dark of sin and shine your holy light. Thank you and amen.

92.

Loving God, I look out my window and see a chipmunk resting at the top of my sweet pea teepee, surveying my front garden and bathing himself. I look further and see the green hills covered with lush trees and further still the stately mountains. Your creative power quiets my soul. The brightness of the rising sun forces me to avert my eyes. It announces your wisdom, which gives light and needs my respect. How good you are, Lord, to fill the earth with food for your creatures. Grant me the grace to receive your provision with gratitude. Everywhere I look, I find your glory. The flowers, the clouds, even the telephone lines all remind me of your goodness. You share your life with all your creation and are near me wherever I go. Thank you and amen.

93.

Loving God, what you have said is enough. I can put my weight down on your promises, and your words will ground me. You have said to come to you, and I run to you for refuge. You have said to not be afraid, that you will remain near and grant me strength in the distressing and challenging times of my life. I believe you and stand firm against the enemy. You have said that even sorrow will not separate me from your love. In fact, you grow even more precious to me during troubled times. You have said trials will come and burn like fire, but I will not be consumed, and I know this is true. The flame only burns away the dross and purifies the gold. You have said to rest in Jesus and find a forever welcome, and I am safe and secure in your loving embrace. Thank you and amen.

94.

Oh, Holy Lord, Almighty God. I rise early to sing my song of praise to you. Holy, you are, yes, but also full of mercy and approachableness. You are Creator, Savior, and Comforter. Your loved ones adore you, and in our best selves, we live to serve your will. Approachable as you are, you are also mysterious and unknown; the clouds that cover your presence shield me from the glory that would kill me. Keep working in me, making me ready to bear the weight of your glory. You alone are perfectly holy, completely powerful, thoroughly loving, and absolutely pure. Oh Holy Lord, Almighty God, all your creation praises your name: the sun rising red in the east, the fog peacefully hugging the valley, the dogs snoring contentedly, my husband's movements of service in the kitchen, and me, here in my prayer chair, readying myself for the day. Bring peace to those fleeing troubles, comfort to those who have already suffered hardship. Make right your broken, beloved world. In your mercy, I pray, Thank you and amen.

95.

I praise you, Holy God, my heart bows before you, for you are Lord of all. I name you Ruler of infinity and Worthy of adoration. If I am quiet and still. I hear echoes of the heavenly choir singing, "Holy, holy, holy is the Lord." (Revelation 4:8) The Acts and the epistles announce your vast power, the prophets tell of your tender and just salvation, the white-robed martyrs prove your worth, and I join the saints in singing your praise. Holy Trinity, you are a mystery; admit me to your union. Thank you and amen.

96.

I give you honor, great anointed son of great King David. At the perfect time, your rule on earth was revealed, and your purpose recognized: you came to end oppression, free the bound, release me from sin, and establish justice. Come quickly to help me right the wrongs. Bring aid to my poor and needy soul. Provide me the courage to be strong, even when I feel weak. Turn my sadness into a song meant only for your ears. Turn on lights, so my way is not shrouded in darkness. Remind me of how precious I am to you. Rain upon my thirsty heart, and like spring flowers, birth the fruit of the spirit in my life. Let your peace and righteousness reign in this broken earth, beginning with us who call ourselves your children. Your name is Love, unchanging and unending. Come rule, great anointed king. Thank you and amen.

97.

Oh, my loving Father, your faithfulness to your beloved is constant, never varying or fading. Your tender mercy never fails. This is who you always have and will always be. Every season, every day brings you glory; the turning leaves, even the dying flowers, offer you praise and tell of your faithfulness and your loving plan for all creation. Of the innumerable blessings you give, these are the ones I'm especially grateful for today: forgiveness, unalterable peace, your encouraging presence, your guiding Spirit, promised strength for today's tasks, and the hope of eternity. You are so kind. You offer me new mercies each morning when I wake; you've already provided for my daily needs. I receive all you offer. Thank you and amen.

98.

Sad today, though I am, my hope is not shaken, for it is founded on God. He awakes my trust this morning, on this day when my new normal begins—the mysterious Holy calls my heart to be its own. Hide me in your temple, hold me in your home, powerful God. Your goodness lasts forever, and your wisdom is deep. The rising sun reminds me that light and splendor surround you; you say the word, and new worlds rise and give you glory. You make all things beautiful. Every day finds my life gifted from your abundance, my soul delighted by your presence, and my path leading to pleasure, joy, and love. All of me gives you thanks: the grieving me and the hopeful me. I am welcome in your heart. Thank you and amen.

99.

You have created a habitation, a city for those you love. You have formed this city with your words and dwell in its midst. It is built on the rock of ages, unshakeable and unassailable. Within its saving walls, I find peace and safety. Within its gates courses a river of living water, sourced by your eternal love. Its graceful flow is constant and dependable. I drink from it, and fear is quieted, courage arises. My home is on its banks. When the sun rises like the fire that guided the Israelites, I know your presence is near and real. When a cloud hovers, granting me shade, I know your protection is mine. Outside the limits of this city, the world clammers and calls, but I will remain within its boundaries, content in your presence. "I'd rather be a doorkeeper..." (Psalm 84:10) Thank you and amen.

100.

I wake early and am glad because I have a lot of things on my list to do today. Let me pursue my work in your name, and may my knowledge of you inform all I think, speak, and do. You've assigned me a role. Let me maintain my cheer as I accomplish my work. In doing my work, I will find your presence and your pleasure. Hide me in your heart and protect me from the snares that lie in wait for me: impatience, pride, discouragement. Accompany me with every word written and spoken. Every conversation exchanged, every dish washed, I offer all my work to your glory. What you have asked of me is not too hard. Your yoke is easy. Let me be mindful of the eternal value of work done obediently; it is preparing me to bear the weight of your glory. Thank you and amen.

101.

Lord, all people long for our world to find some sanity, for justice and kindness to be what rules our actions. Let us put our money where our mouth is and practice kindness toward the neighbor we meet during the day and pray for the good and well-being of the neighbor who is a stranger. Lead us into freedom. As we know peace within our hearts, we can offer peace to one another. Despair threatens our spirits as we hear world news. Oh, loving God, we fix our eyes on you, and hope lifts us out of the fear that would crush us. I admit that prideful ethnocentricity separates me and my country from true justice and peace. Heal me, heal us. You have engraved your character on our hearts. Let us not forget your intention for us is to live in union, love, and peace. Let us live from this intention today. Begin with me. Thank you and amen.

102.

Lord and Father of all humankind, look on us with mercy. Forgive our foolishness, clothe our minds in garments of righteousness, adorn our lives with the purity of service, and beautify our hearts with respect and praise. Let me be content with the simplicity of saying yes to your invitation to follow you, and with the mystery that accompanies your presence. Gently shower me with quietness until I let go of my agitation and worry. I join the silence that filters out stress and striving, leaving an ordered soul marked by the beauty of your peace. Harness my desires and use their energy to serve you. Speak, Lord, I am ready to hear your still small voice of love. Thank you and amen.

103.

Source of all goodness, come. Let the flavor of my life be grace. How could I not return praise for the mercy you have so generously and unflaggingly offered. Teach me the song the angels sing; its theme is your redeeming love. By your help, I come this morning, seeking the treasure of your voice. May your kindness hold me safe throughout the day, just as it has throughout my life. There have been times when I've wandered off into danger, and you have sought me and brought me home. Oh, I owe you such a debt! And yet, all you ask of me is to let you love me well. Here's my heart, Lord. It is yours. Thank you and amen.

104.

I welcome you, King of all creation. Truth be told, I need your help to praise you as I ought. Your name is Father, full of glory; Victor, the risen one; Ruler, before time. I welcome you, word-made flesh. You are the sword of truth; please hear my prayer. Come and grant me your presence. May your word have its way in my life and birth in me holy awe. I welcome you, Spirit of comfort; confirm God's truth in my heart. You are mighty, deserving of my reverence, and your presence is constantly with me. I praise you in your trinitarian fellowship. I see your glory in glimpses now. One day I will see it completely. Until then, I love and adore you in the shadow of heaven. Thank you and amen.

105.

The empty cross, the vacant tomb, love defeating death, that's cause for singing. You are alive now. Bring your healing and salvation to bear on me and this broken world today. Our brokenness causes you to suffer still, but your love rushes in with the hope of life where insult, war, or division threaten death. Holy Spirit, call and keep calling all people to truth and freedom. Jesus, bring your good news this day. Let the earth, the sea, the sky, and all people live in your joy, for your justice, with your love, and to your glory. Thank you and amen.

106.

The birds have their nests, the chipmunks their burrows, but I have the choicest place of refuge and rest: I am held in your arms of love, near your merciful heart. You ensure that my needs are met, and I flourish in your presence. Your protection wraps me round. I am safe, for nothing can separate me from your love. Even sorrow cannot divide us, for you are a man of sorrows and share my grief. You promise to work all things to my good; your plan for transforming me into your holy image is the good I'm heading toward. Thank you and amen.

107.

Lord, I'm a two-talent gal. My ego wishes I were a five-talent girl. But the talents you have given me are gifts from your heart of love, a perfect fit for who I am. I return them to you and thank you for entrusting them to me. May I serve you truly and well, my Lord. Use me to comfort and bless those who mourn, to soothe the weary, to befriend the lonely, to offer the key to freedom to those who are captive, to hold the hand of the lost and lead them home. May my life and work point to Christ, the source of life and peace. Sometimes, Lord, my faith wavers, but my heart is fixed on yours. I love in your name. Thank you and amen.

108.

Lord, grant me the grace to draw close to the outcast, to be brave in the face of toil, to fervently share your love. I need your guarding and your guidance. Take my heart and hold me tight as the uncertainty of the day unfolds. I set out to do your work, add your perfecting touch to my imperfect efforts. May the Spirit's flame inspire my thoughts and deeds; let all I do rise as incense to your throne. By your help and blessing, may I be willing to set aside my will for the sake of the ones you love. Thank you and amen.

109.

Your kingdom is timeless, ever-enduring, ultimately true. Your Spirit brings the wisdom of the Word to my heart and shows me the wonder of Christ's humility. Eternal light dawning upon this finite earth, banishing darkness from this shadowy heart; hope brightens the landscape of my soul. All because of you, Savior, God, merciful one. Thank you and amen.

110.

Lord of my heart, be the lens through which I look at the world. Let all else fade away in comparison to you. Instill good thoughts in my mind today. Let your presence be the light that guides me. Oh, I need your wisdom as I pursue my call. Your word is the guardrail of my life. My loving Father, you are with me always. May I remember to remain with you, love you in return. Holy Spirit, guard my heart, equip me for the work of the day, be the armor that protects me and the power that animates me. I run to you for rest, for a renewed vision, for a picture of glory. Lord, grant me the grace to write for your smile, not for the acclaim of the world; train my heart to desire only your well-done. King of heaven, bright morning star, grant me the grace to enter your joy; whatever happens today, may I cling to you, for you are my heart of hearts. Thank you and amen.

111.

Keep your eyes open, for today God will send you strength as your rudder, power to keep you standing, wisdom as your guide. God's eyes are upon you, God's ears are attuned to you, God's words are spoken to you. God is your friend. Go in the way of God, remain behind the shield of God. Let God be your defender and savior. God's ministering angels stand near, warning off all that would harm you. Keep your eyes open. Thank you and amen.

112.

From all the corners of my life, I come to your table. You've set me a feast: water that sustains my soul, bread that gives me life, the awareness that my sorrow is past and my joy is growing. My dependence on you gains my admittance to the banquet. You sit at the head of the table and invite me to sit with you. You call me friend and speak promises you will keep: forgiveness, freedom, restoration. This feast sustains me. Thank you and amen.

113.

Jesus, great physician, search out all my pain, touch the wounded places with your healing hands, restore my hope, and remove my fear. Cleanse me from the bitterness that robs me of your peace. I've been forgiven much; let me offer forgiveness to all, including myself, for your spirit has shown me the ways I have violated love. Let your peace banish the feelings of guilt that haunt me, the anxiety that unsettles me, and fill me with your joy. Thank you and amen.

114.

Lord, every created thing has a particular gift to offer you: birds, their song; dogs, their wagging tails; me, my heart. Receive it all this morning. We return to you, our source, and our end. Your power proves just and overthrows the oppressor. Your worship and honor begin before time and will never end. From your abundant grace, send refreshment to weary souls. Today, dress me in praise and joy, and let your peace flow from my heart to all whom I meet and all that I undertake. Thank you and amen.

115.

You are the great healer, the one who hears my helpless prayer, I come, asking to be made whole. You will not turn me away. You have cleansed me and named me your beloved daughter, but I sometimes forget my true self and act according to the lies that attempt to hold me captive. The end of this behavior is heaviness and crookedness. Let me look on my bent self with grace and sorrow; let me look into your face of love and stand straight. Standing tall, with eyes fixed on keeping your law of love, I can bear the easy yoke of your gentle and humble ways. Thank you and amen.

116.

Morning has dawned. As the sun rises in glory, so does my heart rise to give you glory. Please, let your glorious power surround me this day. May I say nothing that would injure another; when my anger is triggered, remind me to first look within, at the wound that has been aggravated, before I respond; keep my heart focused on pleasing you, not other people. Use this Lenten discipline to purify my heart so my thoughts and actions proceed from a deep place that is secure in your love. When evening comes, may I be able to point to the ways you walked with me during the trials of this day and how I chose to give you glory. Thank you and amen.

117.

Lord, your words "Let there be light" (Genesis 1:3) spoke creation into being; your words "It is finished" (John 19:30) spoke salvation to humanity. Your words, "Come unto me" (Matthew 11:28) continue to speak life into me, the one you love. Show me the ways I adore you. Thank you that your morning sun burns away the night, in the east and in my heart. Jesus, you are God's glory hidden in plain view; you are God's love expressed in fullness. You were born to overthrow death's hold. You were raised to set me free. Thank you and amen.

118.

Lord, I could sing of your love forever, for you continually bring me to a new, rescued life. I come to you, and you relieve me of my burdens; I come to you, and you set aside my guilt. Your offered blood puts sin to shame; your quiet submission makes the love of God manifest. Oh, if only the world would recognize your amazing love. This daily life of mine drains me. Without your living water, I would run dry. I run to the spring that satisfies. I drink and am renewed. How could I resist your drawing love? How can I show you how much I love you? Thank you and amen.

119.

Forty days and nights, Lord Jesus, you fasted. Forty days and nights, you resisted: unyielding to the temptations the enemy thrusted before you. I join you in your fast, your challenge, your strength. Grant me the grace to stand with you against the tempter's schemes. Let peace rule and gladness rise. Let all your host rejoice. Hold on to me this day; let me not be found unprepared. Thank you and amen.

120.

Jesus, you called yourself the Great Shepherd to describe the nature of our relationship. I can depend upon you to provide for my needs, and you lead me into places where my soul is nourished and refreshed. When I wander, you search for me; your mercy is my guide into truth; your grace lights my path. Death holds no fear for me, for you have taken away its sting. I cling to you when it haunts me. You breathe on me, and I am filled with hope. Fear has lost its footing. The enemies of my soul stand at the edge of my life, unable to interrupt the celebration of our union. I drink from a bottomless cup of blessings, I am marked with your grace, and I remain in your presence throughout my day and days. Your heart is my home; rest and be at peace, oh my soul. Thank you and amen.

121.

Because you love all you've created, all you've created deserves my love and respect. Everyone I meet is precious to you; everyone is a child of your heart, even the ones who have hurt me. Your active love bends, stretches, envelopes both the hurting and the hurter, urging reconciliation and peace. Lord, you've been so tender and merciful toward me. Let me reciprocate your love with tenderness and mercy toward all I meet today. Thank you and amen.

122.

Jesus, you are the way, the way to escape death and its stain, the way to the Father. You are the truth; the wisdom that informs my mind and purifies my heart comes from you. You are the life; your empty tomb proves your vitality and supremacy over death. I trust in you and am safe from death's reach. The Way, the Truth, the Life: grant me the grace to follow your way, to know your truth, and to attain your life. Joy is the fruit of such a gift. Thank you and amen.

123.

Word of life and power, make known the kingdom of our God to all creation. Awaken each one's desire for heaven. Word of strength and purity, the world needs to know you and live in your light, not blind darkness. Wake us, cheer us, charge us to live from love. Call us, empower us, equip us to love well. Lord, may I be filled and formed by your love today. Thank you and amen.

124.

When I wander from your goodness, you welcome me upon my return. You will not leave me desolate and sorrowful, for you are a gracious God. Yes, you allow storms, but you also calm the sea. Your anger is real, but so is your desire to save. The long night of sorrow is almost past; the dawn of joy is on the horizon. I will rise now and greet its coming. With gladness, I face the light. Thank you and amen.

125.

Christ, your wounded heart shows all the world your love. You ask me to share in your love by sharing your cross. I am yours, a gift of the Father. Your love for me will never end. So completely loved, I gladly take your light yoke and bear your burden along with you. Praise you, Father, giver of all gifts; praise you, Jesus, source of life; praise you Spirit, bringer of power. Praise you, Trinity, who chose to dwell within this temple; make it holy by your presence. Thank you and amen.

126.

Lord, I look to saints who have faithfully gone before me as models for living the Kingdom life. Remembering Joseph, spouse of Mary, I recount his honest and obedient responses to your call on his life. He was faithful to the mysterious trust you asked of him. He cared for Mary and Jesus through uncertain times. May I follow your call and carry with me the ones you've given me to love even when I don't understand why you're leading in such a manner; may my trust in you trump my reason. Thank you and amen.

127.

Lord Jesus, the foundation of my hope is your death and living holiness. Nothing else can bear the weight of my trust. When it seems your presence is hidden, my heart rests on the faith I have in your constant grace. My hope is anchored to your resurrected life. No storm or wind can separate us. Clinging to your promise, remembering your spilled blood, holds me fast when troubles arise. Though my mind and habits would break faith with you, your faithfulness hangs on to me. For you are the solid rock, all else is melting snow. Thank you and amen.

128.

Oh Lord, single source of hope, giver of the great well-done, listen to your world's cry and receive our praise. I admit my lack of holiness, my violations of love, the shame that rests over my soul, and my great need for your cleansing. Come, let your spirit transform my mind from dark to light, my words from judgment to encouragement, and my deeds from self-centered to serving others. Cast my sins behind you, remember them no longer, let your forgiveness be foremost on my mind, not my lack of holiness. Restore me through your mercy. In your loving care, through your righteousness, I rest and pray. Receive my Lenten sacrifice as proof of my heart's desire to love you more. Thank you and amen.

129.

How appropriate that you were mistaken for a gardener on that first Sunday morning because you are, indeed, a gardener of souls. Sow seeds of life into the hearts of all who seek you. It makes sense that you were unrecognized in that dawn light, for your presence often surprises and comes in unexpected ways. But your voice, calling my name, telling me the truth, penetrates my unknowing and misguided expectations and bids my heart to come close. I call you my teacher. You call me your messenger. Thank you and amen.

130.

Oh, my soul, start afresh right now. Trust God to guide you; place all your confidence in God's constant nearness. You are not alone; the Spirit lives within you, granting you strength and hope. Today's agenda is unknown, so build your trust in God's unchanging love. It is the rock, not the sand, and it will stand firm, not crumble. Dare to be still and wait on his lead. Let your heart be hopeful and content. He has always come through. Your Father knows your deepest desires, and his love will give you exactly what you need. Keep cheerful while you wait. Serve joyfully, for your trust teaches you that God will not abandon you. Thank you and amen.

131.

Dear always-present Christ, you are my king, creator, and Lord. Receive my humble praise this morning. In your cross, I find a grace: the nails in your hands punctured the bubble of sin that kept me captive. I can now follow you in freedom. The earth trembled at your death. The sun grew dark as you drew your last breath. You, who created the stars that light the night yet hid your own light behind the flesh of a man, you deigned to bear the weight of the human burden, sharing in our humanity so we can share in your victory. Now you sit in the glory of your Father. Conqueror of death, defend me, reign in my heart anew and afresh. Thank you and amen.

132.

Oh, Lord, you are my bread for the coming day, my food as I venture out into the work you've given me to do. I acknowledge you and know you are the strength I need for the day set before me. Jesus, you reveal God's love; you bind my heart in unity with my brothers and sisters. In you, I hope; in you, I have the promise of eternity. You are the source of love and truth. My heart is restless until it rests in you, where doubts are quieted, empty yearnings vacated, and my true self finds it true peace. You feed me and fill me with light and joy; mystery though you are, you are my sure guide to justice, peace, contentment, and eternal bliss. Thank you and amen.

133.

You are alive, Jesus. You have bought me, and I am yours. What a confident hope that offers! Once you were dead, and now you lead me into life. Victor over death, you live to save me this very moment. Let me hold this truth through all my moments. Hush my fears and capture my tears. My heart quakes in anticipation of the day; calm me with your presence and your breath. You went through all you did to give me life. You have gone ahead of me to prepare the day, and you will walk with me through it. I am safe and useful in your hands. Thank you and amen.

134.

Oh, my soul, turn toward God, your perfect parent, with words and a posture of praise. May my thoughts, my emotions, and my will all conspire to bless God's holy name. I remember the way his mercy surprised me, so I will focus not on my sin, but on the manifold forgiveness I've been given. Thank you, Lord, for sustaining the life within my body and for the healing process of my heart. Broken though I was, you kindly saved me from destruction. Even today, you separate me from my sin, as far as the east is from the west. Like a perfect father, your compassion has no beginning nor end. Shower me with your mercy; let it pour out upon my children and grandchildren. Your kingdom come. Thank you and amen. [A prayer based on Psalm 103]

135.

Holy Spirit, the curator of perfect peace, put at holy ease this anxious heart of mine; speak calm to the agitated sea of insecurity, and hold my life in tranquil stillness today. Holy Spirit, presence of God's perfect love, shine in my heart; may your empowering and purifying fire spark every noble and true desire within me and burn away all the ego-focused embers. Holy Spirit, giver of God's perfect joy, fill my heart with gladness; for as spring renews the face of the earth, you renew my hope and assurance that all will be well. Thank you and amen.

136.

Oh, holy God, my breath reminds me that you are the source of my life. Breathe on me and grant me a fresh beginning this morning. Teach my heart to love the things you care about; train my will to act according to love's demands. Spirit of God, release the holy within me; be the trellis upon which I climb. As I depend on you, show forth the beauty of the true me. May I blossom and bear fruit fit for eternity, in your name and for your glory. Thank you and amen.

137.

Lord, it is your great desire for every person to know of your great love and to live a life overflowing with joy, contentment, and provision; toward that end, you trust me to carry this great news to the world you so love. Grant me the grace to communicate the hope of new life; may my words remind people of their true worth, my actions give them no reason to doubt their value. Form my mind to think of each person I encounter today as your precious child, and then to offer them the same love and respect you offer me. You've poured such love into my heart, have so eagerly forgiven all my sins, from the slight to the great. You've so generously given me new mercies every morning. What I have received, I give away. I find joy and peace in such a manner of living, and the world is drawn closer to your heart of love because of my witness. Thank you and amen.

138.

Oh, my loving, perfect parent, I approach the door of your house and find you running toward me, arms outstretched, a welcoming smile upon your face. In your merciful embrace, my sins and my betrayals of your love melt away. They are inconsequential as I remain locked in the joy of homecoming. Why do I forget your door is always open—that you are the only true guide to peace and well-being? When joy seems far away and despair or discouragement too close, help me be a quicker student of grace and remember that your door is always open and your ear is always ready to hear. Thank you and amen.

139.

I look out on all you have created and all whom you've re-created and bless your name; Jesus, you show us the image of the Father and the power of the Spirit. Love compelled you to take on human form, making the way for our brokenness to be made whole. That same creative love took pity on our sin-soaked state and faced the cross to wash us clean. Oh my Lord, for my freedom, you bore the wounds, felt the spear pierce your side; let me never forget the price your love paid for my release. Thank you and amen.

140.

Lord, may my words bring encouragement to the ones you've given me to love. Fill me with the Holy Spirit so that I may empty myself in service. Grant me the grace to be generous with the many resources you've given me, to seek out the misunderstood, to have patience with the young, to call out the giftedness in those around me. Lord, may I share your sorrow and joy. My faith in you holds me steady until the day when I no longer need it. For, on that day, I will see you in your perfection and be a many-faceted diamond, catching and reflecting your beauty from every angle. Thank you and amen.

141.

Don't forget, oh my soul, your God is committed to saving you. There is no need for fear. The Lord is on your side and protects you. His saving grace is sitting next to you even now. So dare to be glad; drink from the spring of living, healing water; and sing of God's refreshing mercy. Your Lord has done great deeds within you and for you; you have no need to be shy about telling your friends and family about them! Praise God's name, lift your voice in song for the holy and humble one has come to dwell in your midst. Thank you and amen.

142.

Jesus, you are such a great friend to me. I come to you with all my worries and concerns, and you take them from my burdened heart; there is nothing that is not made bearable when I share it with you. Talking with you about the cares of my life relieves me of anxiety and sorrow. There will be things along my path today that will tempt me to doubt your love and goodwill; guard me against their lure. Jesus, you know me intimately. You know the turns in the road where I'm likely to go off course; remind me in those moments that you are near and hold me steady. There is much in the world and in my life that could immobilize me, among them relationships that challenge my patience and kindness. In these times, Lord, I will run to you. Your strong arms will protect and provide. Be my power to carry on, my refuge when I'm misunderstood, my comfort when I sorrow. You are my true friend. Thank you and amen.

143.

Lord, I look out on this fresh morning, and I see your mighty works all around: the mountains rising in the horizon, the river that makes its way to the sea, the pale blue sky with splashes of white cloud. Even the buildings that have been crafted by humankind are the result of your generative power. Your wisdom created the rhythm of day and night; your goodness filled the earth with food and created animals for our enjoyment and use. I cannot help but see your wonderful hand everywhere I look. You give a hint of yourself in all you've created: your beauty in the roses, your terror in the snake, your power in the wind. You are hidden in all creation. You are the source of life, and we are in your care. Everywhere I go today, in all I undertake, you will be with me. Thank you and amen.

144.

Come, from every corner of the earth, for our Lord has set a magnificent table. It is laden with bread that supplies truth and life, fruit that fills us with joy and empties us of sorrow, and water that sustains us for the day. Come, you who love the Lord, the feast is prepared. Come, receive the fulfilled promise! God's plan for you is sure and steady. At God's word, the old chains that bound you will erode and fall away. You are welcome to the table; you are forgiven all sins, big and small, and freed from all forms of death, so learn to live. A seat of honor has been reserved for you, for you are a friend of the King. Come, taste, and see that the Lord is good. Thank you and amen.

145.

Mercy called my name, invited me into the school of love. She taught my heart, bent toward death, to stretch toward life. I was bound for destruction until she opened my mind to the glory of your name. Grace opened the door and ushered me into freedom, where in response to your choice of me, I chose you. I owe grace endless thanks, for I know you now, and you are my highest hope and the quenching of all my thirsts. My love for you is as true as my imperfection allows and proves your initiating love. Oh Seeker and Giver, thank you and amen.

146.

When I need you, you are my help. When despair threatens, you are my hope. When storms rage, you are my refuge. You are my safe house and forever home. Where you reign, there is security and protection from the assault of enemies. I remember that you are eternal. You were before the earth was created; my long days and years are but a night watch in your sight. Time passes, circumstances change, but you remain the same. You have helped me in the past. You are my hope in what's to come. You will be with me in the hours of this day and walk me to my eternal home. Thank you and amen.

147.

I bless you, creator of light. The morning is filled with your brilliance; it chases away darkness and death. I woke this morning with uncertainty about the day. There is a fear that haunts me like a forgotten dream. Hear my heart's prayer, especially the one that has no words. Apart from your mercy, I would sink into numbness, and my day would be empty and marked by irritation; instead, let me feed on your grace. Awaken me to the gifts of this day, the hope of newness, and the unfolding of your story in and through me. This is the day you have made. I will rejoice and be glad. Thank you and amen.

148.

Eternal God, creator of all things, you are the one who made our earth's rhythm: the day and night, the changing seasons, the sun and rain. All are ordered and sustained by your rule and way so. You look on humankind and know the intent of our hearts. Those determined to promote their own agenda at the cost of harming others will reap what they have sowed: condemnation. But Lord, have mercy on me; save me from myself, for I call on you. Come, be my champion, defend me and arm me with your strength. Teach me to heed your gentle prompts; lead me in paths made safe by your goodwill. I will be tempted to wander off. When this happens, remind me of my hope: your smiling welcome and the words, Well done. Your grace is my supply. Thank you and amen.

149.

Lord Jesus, the prophets told of your coming light, and John, the baptizer, pointed you out: "the lamb who takes away the sin of the world." (John 1:29) You who came to cleanse the world of sin deigned to be washed in the water of baptism. May I live worthily of such humility and love. My baptism marks me as a citizen of heaven. It quietly reminds me that I am one with you, and you share your identity with me. I am the Father's beloved child in whom he is well pleased. Such awareness generates praise within me. May I live as I am named. Thank you and amen.

150.

Oh God, my limited vocabulary is insufficient to express the praise you are due for your amazing love. But I offer you what I am able: awe at the gifts you daily send, thanks for the countless blessings, gratitude for mercy, ever-new. This morning, I lift my heart and wait for your gracious word of love. Selah. Receive the love I offer as I tell you my heart's desires. Grant me your smile as I willingly serve you today. Whether the hour holds moments of delight or difficulty, I will trust your love and praise you in joy and tedium. Open my eyes to catch your beauty in my home and outside my door; increase my faith in your good and glorious will. May my obedience make my life a container of joy and praise. Thank you and amen.

151.

I praise you, Lord of all! I enter your presence through the gifts you've given: in you, I am found and brought home, my brokenness is made whole, shame has been lifted from my head, and forevermore my sins are forgiven. Your grace sought me; your favor found me when I needed rescue. You are slow to anger and quick to bless. I praise you for your faithfulness. Like a perfect parent, your attention is always on my well-being. You know my frailty and carry me when I tire. You rescue me from all internal and external enemies—Alleluia and praise you. Your mercy is constant. Thank you and amen.

152.

I trust myself to you, Lord Jesus, son of Mary, son of God. I come to you this morning, with my soul bent. Help me to belong to none other than you. The gates of the Kingdom are open, and I am welcome. This is my home, the source of my power. In leaving heaven and coming to earth, you brought hoped-for light to our darkness. Satisfy my every hunger, strengthen the weak areas of my soul, and liberate the areas bound by pride. Lord, let me think rightly about myself; I am broken and beautiful, a beloved sinner. Teach me to say no to death, to love and serve well, and to seek first the Kingdom that is my true home. Thank you and amen.

153.

Oh Lord, I count myself among the saints who are learning to cooperate with your grace; I join with them and bless your name. How could I not? You faced down death and rose from the grave so that

I may share your crown. May I wear it with dignity and offer grace to all I encounter today: all people, all creatures, and all situations. I pray to reflect your radiance to the world you've given me to love. There are things I do not understand, mysteries that seem unsolvable, questions that remain unanswered, yet I trust you will set all things right. Grant me the grace to hold faith in your time and plan. Thank you and amen.

154.

The sins of the world are like a brutal, vicious, arrogant army, marching against the holiness of God. They are the hammer that pounded the nails into your hands and feet, the soldier's lance that pierced your side. Their weapons deal death to you and to me, but your death won me life! From your wounds flow grace, by your stripes we are healed. With each blow, you absorbed our sins; now I can approach your holiness and join you in defeating death. May I march for peace where there is disharmony and bring truth to the lies that blind people to the value of each individual, themselves included. Thank you and amen.

155.

There is so much noise in the world, in my life, it is hard to quiet myself enough to hear and recognize your voice. The loud roar of today's urgents, the nagging whisper of shoulds, and the enticing lure of mindlessness: are they your invitation to action, or do they mask your good plan for my day? The way through this confusion is to begin by being still in the light of your word. A phrase in Psalm 145:6 dazzles me: "I will proclaim your great deeds." This defines my day. I will look for opportunities to announce your goodness; this priority will determine what I do this day. Of all the urgents and shoulds, which can I undertake that will make known your greatness? I will trust my inclination and approach the day with confidence that I am heeding your voice. Thank you and amen.

156.

Lord, no thing, no one, comes close to your perfection. Your loving action on my behalf is the wonderful story I will spend my life learning to trust. You have saved me time and again through the kindness of friends and through the betrayal of so-called friends. Be my Lord and reign in my life. You are constantly working to set your people free. Free me—feed me with your love. Bring me safely to a place where I am guarded by your grace, at home with you. Through me, invite others to come home to you as well. Be my Lord and reign in my life. Thank you and amen.

157.

When things of this world seem chaotic and without direction, I take great comfort in knowing that your kingdom and goodwill never change. You spoke order into the chaos once and even now are pulling the good and beautiful out of the muck into the light of your love. You humbly entered the muck, bringing rescue to all souls who will take your outstretched hand. Pull me into your light, brilliant Sun. Place in me the hope that does not dim; wake me from the dark dream that blinds me, my Savior, my God. Thank you and amen.

158.

Lord, you have not left me without a witness to your holiness. My conscience troubles me and tells me I've come short of your law of love. I have sought comfort over service, and judgment over compassion. Grant me the grace of your cleansing word, and eliminate the stain of sin from my life. Oh Lord, with you there is forgiveness, and with your pardon, there is no condemnation. Let my conscience align with your declaration over me. I am your beloved child, in whom you are well pleased. This identity forms my heart, and from my heart flows the love of Christ. May it hold me throughout this day and into eternity. Thank you and amen.

159.

Your mercy called my name and spoke to me in a language I understood. My heart and mind were charmed by sin until mercy taught me their falseness and revealed your glory to my awakened heart. Your love chose me. Grace set me free so that I could choose you in return. Now, may your loving patience teach me to choose the virtuous crown of the Spirit above all the flashy trinkets of the world. Oh Initiator of Love, thank you and amen.

160.

Every creature brings its unique style of praise to honor you, my King: the birds, their chirping; the squirrels, their clicking; the dogs, their wagging, and me, my still heart that knows you are God. At your birth, angels filled the sky with songs of wonder. Grant me the grace to hear their chorus this morning and join in their anthem! Amen.

Loving God, may your power prove right the cause of justice, and bring down the proud oppressor. This is your forever theme; continue writing this story in and through me. Lord, this world needs the renewing rain of your Spirit. My thirsty soul needs the refreshing dew of your grace. May the promise of that one day be mine this day. May joy and praise be my clothing. May peace flow from your throne to restless places and hearts on this precious earth. Thy Kingdom come. Thank you and amen.

161.

Lord, I must admit this morning, my soul feels parched. As dew falls on the grass in the morning, surprise me with your refreshing presence. As light fills the room at the flip of a switch, fill me with the joy of the Holy Spirit. My hope is not in vain; you will give me yourself in the breaking of the word, in the quiet of my breath, in the stillness of my heart. You will quench my thirst and lighten my dreariness. I will be still and know that you are God. Thank you and amen.

162.

Jesus, you once stood on a boat at the shore's edge, lifting your voice with words of wisdom and hope. You were winsome and compelling. Your words offered the promise of life; your presence emanated power, and crowds drew close. Today, I draw close to hear the same invitation to wholeness. You graciously make room for me and receive me with gladness. If I were healthy, I would not need a physician, but I am injured and need your healing; I am weak and want your power. This morning, this moment is the perfect time! Come, my soul's great physician, release your restoring power, and let me know your saving power. Now, on this day of celebration and sorrow, come. Thank you and amen.

163.

Loving God, your work did not stop after you created the world; you labor still maintaining the beauty and order of the earth. All are held by your good and gracious will. All the stretches of my mind's imagination are known by you: the farthest star, the tiniest speck of sand. Your care reaches all that has breath. Even the lowly sparrow has you as a friend. The earth is full of your glory, the vast sea tells of your power, the endless sky whispers your wisdom. Without words, the dahlias outside my window sing your praise, and the fresh breeze reminds me of your renewing presence. Lord, let me, like your glorious creation, depend upon you for provision and energy and declare your goodness with wordless joy. Thank you and amen.

164.

Jesus, you are the one who intercedes for us and who paid the ransom for our freedom. Heavenly Father, thank you for the gift of your son. The mystery of your love always holds me captive. I join with all the children of the heavenly King, singing praise to our glorious Father as we trod the path that leads to our perfection. We follow the signposts left by the saints who have gone before us to our home in God. They've entered their promised rest. Loving Lord, teach me to rest as I walk. The day before me holds endless glimpses of your glory. Train my eyes to find you, hiding in plain sight. The day before me offers countless opportunities to cooperate with grace. May I live in the awareness of the choices set before me: life or death. I am walking the path that leads to my perfect home. Lord, mercifully keep me on course. Thank you and amen.

165.

Lord of mercy, always kind, I come seeking your mercy. Tainted by sin, I enter the cleansing water of your presence. I fall short of my own expectations of righteousness and berate my lack, but it is against you alone that I have sinned, and your judgment names me guilty and forgiven. You absorb my sin and leave me a clean heart and a new mind. May your Spirit grant me joy and support as I walk with a fresh start today. Thank you and amen.

166.

Lord, there is a hunger in my heart that is not satisfied by things; if ignored, it becomes greedy. I try to feed it with food, with entertainment, with possessions or acclaim, hoping to satisfy its demands, yet it remains empty. Its satisfaction cannot be accomplished through anything other than prayer and faith. You are the true Bread of Heaven I seek, the godly Life I hunger for, the eternal food that daily satisfies. It is your presence my heart desires, and in finding you, my heart can rest. All I need and all I want are satisfied in you. I can be still and know that you are God. I taste and see that you are good. Thank you and amen.

167.

Jesus, it is by your death that I live; your very self is my daily bread. You gave all and continue to give all. You are truly the giver and the gift; your life is the hallmark and the source of love. How can I thank you, Lord, for your loving-kindness? I give you my heart, my strength, and my mind. As imperfect as they are, I offer them sincerely. Take,

Lord, and receive my life. I pray I will be a gift and a giver to the world you've given me to love. Thank you and amen.

168.

Oh Jesus, wherever love lives, you are there, bringing joy to the hearts of the lover and the loved, imparting peace even in the midst of challenging situations. You are my source of life, and you shed light upon my rejoicing spirit. Thank you for your constancy. You always listen for my call, save me from my worst self, and are good to me at all times. You are my all in all. When I seek you, I find you in all I undertake, even in the bread and water I enjoy. My heart is restless, my routine changeable; your presence is the stillness and the guidance I desire. I look to you for the day ahead, confident in your care for me and whatever the day holds. Thank you and amen.

169.

At one time, I spread my people out among foreigners, and now I gather them up, protecting them as a gardener does her prize roses. I will buy back my child. I will trade myself for her return from defeat. She shall climb high, shouting with joy. She will rush to receive the blessings I have for her: nourishment, joy, health, meaningful work, and strength. I have built an irrigation system into the garden of her life. I will always water her, never will she wither from lack of rain. I will sing a tune that calls out her youth to dance and her wisdom to smile in gladness. I will turn her places of sadness into joy, and she will know comfort and hope after her sorrow. I will generously provide her with opportunities for ministry and service. She will overflow with my favor. This is what the Lord says about me. Thank you and amen. [A prayer based on Jeremiah 31:10-14]

170.

Because God rescues and heals me, I shall practice trust and set aside my fear. For you, oh Lord, stand between me and death. You are nearer than the air around me. Pause and breathe, knowing I am on the way to complete restoration. Cause joy to bubble within me, snippets of praise songs resting under my breath. Your mercy is new this morning. Lord, thank you that you have set up your camp within me; your renovation of my heart is a thing of beauty. Thank you and amen.

171.

Praise you, Lord Jesus, for your kindness leads to repentance and the renewing of my strength and hope. I trust you, the image of the Father, shepherd of my soul, to find me when I wander and bring me home. Your glance reveals my brokenness. Your gaze heals my selfishness and pride; your smile releases my beauty. Touch the wounds, comfort the griefs, forgive the wrongs, kindle the love. For you are my hope in the dark, my dawn breaking with light and splendor. Thank you and amen.

172.

Oh Lord of Love, grant my restless mind the gift of your peace. Calm the interior churning of my thoughts and plans so I can hear your quiet, whispered words of love. Grant me the grace to walk in the light of your humility. Enlarge my compassion and power. Let me be quick to respond and ready to serve. Oh, Great Physician, use my words to heal the broken. Seeker of the Lost, through my kindness, offer an invitation to return home to those who have wandered. Forgiving Judge, may my life display your power to release those chained within captivity. Lord of Love, grant this broken world peace. Thank you and amen.

173.

Our lives often feel crowded and busy yet empty; unchecked, we demand our privileges and preferences. We fill our days with strivings for self's advantage. Lord, break into our days with your humble voice asking us to trust you. Lord, where need abounds, where fear reigns, where greed consumes, may your tears wash us clean. Permit neither our helplessness, sorrows, burdens, nor hunger to push you away. Lord, fill our cups with your grace, and then in your name, let us offer cups of fresh water to the thirsty souls around us. Come, walk among us with healing, comfort, and peace. Thank you and amen.

174.

Who you are: the loved only-begotten Son, the adored Living Word, the One who lives forever, the powerful and merciful Lord. What you did: brought me salvation and life by defeating death and sin through your own dying. What I ask: save me today as you have saved me forever. What I do: walk in the shadow of your cross to enjoy the light of your life. Thank you and amen.

175.

Lord Jesus Christ, I can count on you to be beside me, a companion: ahead of me, a guide, behind me, a defender. You are the king of my heart. Lord and Savior, be within me, a magnet pulling me home; be below me, the foundation of my life; and be above me, the umbrella that covers me in trouble. I can trust you will never depart from me. Jesus, on my right hand, ordering my mind; on my left hand, inspiring my creativity; and all around me, highlighting the beauty of creation. I carry your name with me into strife. Christ, you, who lie down with me while I sleep, rest beside me as I sit. Await me when I wake. You are the light of my life. Thank you and amen. (This prayer is a nod to St. Patrick!)

176.

I greet you this morning—you who traded your life for mine, you who is king and lord of all! Interceder, Lamb of God, yours is the right to take the throne, for your rule brings peace that never ends. King of Truth and Power, shed your light upon this darkened world. Raise up transformed lives that seek to live for your Kingdom's sake. Let your peace rule in individual hearts, and may this peace be the norm, not the exception. Spread your peace among nations so together we can sing, "Praise to you Jesus Christ, King and Lord of earth and sea Calvary crowned you as King of Love." Come rule us, beginning with me. Thank you and amen.

177.

Come, Lord Jesus! I invite you to enter the doors of my heart as my welcomed guest, my gracious master, my beloved friend, and my honored Lord. Just as you changed the water to wine at Cana, say the word and change me; transform my needs and doubts into newborn hope and joy reignited. Awaken my faith, surprise my dullness, and increase my belief in your desire to give me the best I can imagine. You have loved me with a constant love; I seek you in the hidden places and find you buried in plain sight within my heart and in the hearts of those you've given me to love. Grant me the grace to believe that heaven has drawn near. Thank you and amen.

178.

I have only one voice, and with it, I will praise you. You are the one who returns me to a normal that is new and vibrant, the one who is brilliant with kindness, the one who, though I am wayward and stubborn, wins my heart by your patient and generous pursuit. Holy Spirit, my voice is not strong; its tone is not clear, so I need your accompanying harmony to transform it into a beautiful melody that honors your name. Lord Jesus, when I focus on you, my fear subsides, my sorrow diminishes, and life, health, and peace are magnified. For your sake, you canceled my sin; for my sake, you set me free from sin—you are enough for me! My one voice joins the countless voices that sing your praise this day and from now on. Thank you and amen.

179.

Lord, Jesus, when I am lost, you are my GPS. When I am confused, seeking your way brings me clarity. When bound by poor habits, obeying your good will brings me freedom. You grant me a vision of a good life; your voice speaks hope to my numbed heart. Listening to your Spirit pulls me from the danger of wrong choices. You, Lord of all, came to serve your creation, to search out the ones who live in shame and grant them favor. May my life today reveal the power of your cross, for in letting my false self die, my true self rises. Thank you and amen.

180.

God, you are the one who keeps me safe. You never weaken in your defense of me; even when I am ill and unpleasant company, you stay close with help at the ready. The wily one, the enemy of my soul, throws daggers of defeat against me, tempting me to give in to the taunts toward despair. But when I do, I have forgotten that the war has been won, that you are the victor, and that I can maintain my hope. Oh Lord, grant me the grace to remember that you have found me, you know me, and you hold me close and empower me. I will trust in the Lord. Thank you and amen.

181.

Dear Jesus, I recognize the power that is available to me when I call on your name in my times of need. I join the universe in returning the bounty of your blessings; I choose you as my Lord and King. Your saving grace is generous and ready to save all who call on your name. Let all people hear your name and respond to your invitation and join creation in praising your name. One day, we'll see you face to face; on that day, we'll offer you the crowns of beauty we've worn by your grace and goodness. Until then, I give you my allegiance, my body, and my will. Thank you and amen.

182.

You can return and rest, my soul, for the Lord is near and will give you strength to bear the load this day brings. You can trust your God to order your hours and to provide all you need. Rest your confidence on this: God intends to guide you into greater life. Set your hope on this: God reveals himself as you walk by faith. Today's unknowns shall one day be understood. It is yours to trust that all will be well and to act in love as Jesus did, by God's grace and power. Thank you and amen.

183.

My soul quietly waits for you, Lord. You have proven yourself worthy over and over. You alone are my defense and my power; in quiet and trust, I am shielded and secure. My future is safe with you, my refuge, my guard. You have a plan; I need not worry. I can rely on you with confidence and entrust the most precious secrets of my heart, for I am precious to you. Your word has been said; your wonders have proven your intention to release me into perfection. Always kind, let me return your kindness with works of love. Thank you and amen.

184.

You once broke loaves and miraculously fed thousands; now, break open your word, the bread of life, and feed my spirit. As you blessed the bread before you gave it to the hungry, bless me so that I can be broken and given to the hungry in my small world. I read your word and seek freedom-granting truth. Send your Spirit to teach me the ways of truth, the actions of love, and the joy of freedom. Thank you and amen.

185.

Our Father, lead us in the way of peace. Without your guidance, we wander off the true and living path and into brambles of doubt and sorrow. Lead us in the way of truth. Without your direction, our minds are easily lost in erroneous thinking and habitual despair or apathy. Lead us in the way of righteousness; be our companion and nudge us toward justice, mercy, and humility. Lead us to the place of salvation and strength. The road may be steep, the terrain pleasant or treacherous, yet we will trust your good will—our perfection is in Christ. Thank you and amen.

186.

I thank you, God, from my heart, with my will and my mind, for you accomplish wonderful things on my behalf, and I am glad in you. It was your love that carried me as a baby in my mother's arms, your goodness that walked with me during my youth, and your power that energizes me for the life I lead this day. Continue near me, generous God. Grant me your joy and peace. When I am perplexed, give me clarity, and when I am tempted to forget your faithfulness, send me reminders that you are my true satisfaction. All praise to you, Father, Son, and Holy Spirit. Thank you and amen.

187.

Oh, love that will never let me go, I feel weighed down by deadlines and demands. Resting in you is the source of my peace. I give you my worries and fears; I sink down into ocean depths of your love and trust that I will rise enriched and equipped. Oh light that knows all my ways, I join the wick of my flickering life to the flame of your constant light and burn brighter and more true. Oh joy that draws near in my distress, my heart claims your promise of empowering me for your service. Oh cross that proves love conquers all, my pride must die so that love can reign. I offer you my life this day. Thank you and amen.

188.

The love of Christ runs deeper than the ocean, wider and higher than the expanse of heaven. That he took the form of humanity for the sake of love goes way beyond the capacity of my imagination! For our sake, he was baptized, fasted, and faithfully said no to the tempter's tricks. For us, he suffered betrayal, the humiliation of a thorny crown, and gave his last breath. For us, he defeated death, rose to life, and reigns above all. For us, the Spirit was sent to guide, empower, and comfort. Praise and thanks to you Jesus, God, and Holy Spirit. Thank you and amen.

189.

Oh my soul, praise the King of heaven. To him, I bring my gratitude. His life bought the ransom for mine; his wounds brought the healing of mine. His completeness brings me wholeness; his forgiveness sets me free. I will always have reason to praise him! Jesus, when I am in distress, your grace reminds me I belong to you, that your favor rests upon me, and that my heart can calm down. You are slow to chide and quick to bless; you have my best at heart always. You are a merciful parent, caring for my needs, protecting me from unknown harm; you know my weaknesses and carry me when my strength fails. Angels who look at your face, sun, moon, and all creation bow down and adore the God of Grace. Thank you and amen.

190.

Your faithfulness is more vast than the spreading sky, oh God, my creator; your love is the constancy I depend upon. Kindness and compassion mark your presence in my life. I can count on your unchanging grace. Each morning, I wake to new mercies; each evening, I can recall how you have provided all I need. All creation reminds me of your faithfulness: the gentle rain, the lightening sky, and the chirping birds all join my song of praise. And the greatest gift all: sin and its stain are replaced with peace and freedom as I let you guide my choices. Come, Holy Spirit, form my heart to praise my savior. Thank you and amen.

191.

Oh forever living God, you have given yourself to me. What delight! All satisfactions that temporarily fulfill the longings of my body and soul point me to you, the one who satisfies completely. There have been moments when I've witnessed your glory, and at those times, nothing compares with your love. I lift my hands and heart to give you praise. Feed my soul now with a feast that will not disappoint. You are the help of my life. I take shelter under your spreading branches and find joy and purpose in your protection. Thank you and amen.

192.

Come, heart of mine, come, and recognize the countless ways God cares for you. Winter is passing, and the spring-hinting earth reminds me that life, even my life, will be renewed. I come this morning with thanks. I am your garden. May I bear the fruit of praise; gently but thoroughly weed out the invasive, death-spreading vines that would choke the life and beauty from my soul. Where weed and flower intertwine, grant me the patience to trust your wisdom. You will do what's best for your garden. Gather me as a bundle of fragrant flowers. May I add beauty to your temple. Thank you and amen.

193.

Dear Jesus, my strength for the daily battle against death, you have shared your power so that I may grab on to life and experience its joy and victory. By your grace, I will run the race set before me, looking to you, the source and goal of my faith. I cast my cares upon you. For guidance through the day, I depend upon you; for provision each hour, I rest upon your mercy. Fear be gone, my Lord is near; his promise is true, and he calls me his beloved. Lord, I believe; help my unbelief. Thank you and amen.

194.

Today, I may get off course or not recognize the landmarks that guide me toward home, so won't you take my hand and walk me through this day? You who exchanged your life for mine, hold me in your powerful hand, for I am weak, and you are mighty. Strengthen me, Bread of Heaven, for the life you've blessed. Heal me, Living Water, so I may bless others. Lead me, Fire and Cloud, so I may bless your name. Always and in all things. Thank you and amen.

195.

Lord, hear my prayer: I long to love you more completely. When I find myself restless or anxious, when my mind is consumed with coming off as perfect, when I am working way too hard to appear impressive, these are sure signs that I am looking for temporary fixes for my broken soul. Trusting only you to give what is best leads to peace and rest. Whatever comes my way, may my heart say, "How can this help me love you more completely?" Grant me the grace to seek you always and in all things. Thank you and amen.

196.

Lord, one step at a time is all that is asked of me. It's always been true but seems even more true this morning than it did yesterday. With my heart fixed on your love, I can walk as you lead, where you lead, through whatever circumstances you allow, I am convinced nothing can separate me from your love. In fact, all things can draw me into your love more completely. It is by faith I walk this path. I walk it with you by my side, trusting your love. Thank you and amen.

197.

Lord, for the most part, I live in the amazing peace of knowing you are holding my life and my future, but there are moments when my heart quakes with doubt and worry. When these moments come upon me, make me like a weaned child: one who is pleased with being held on your lap, not worrying about the next hour, content with the joy of the present. A well-cared-for child assumes she will be carried when she's weary, fed when she's hungry, protected from harm; and I am your well-cared for daughter. I am perfectly safe in your arms, my guard and my guide. Prove your boundless love in and through me. Thank you and amen.

198.

Oh Love that holds me close and will never let me go, my grateful and weary heart rests in your presence. Giver of Life, I give my life back to you. Lower me into the ocean of your kindness, and lift me up into a life enriched and overflowing with gratitude. Oh Light that encompasses me, I join my flickering flame to yours, and by your grace, I will blaze like the sun. Oh, Joy that sought in me the dark, I receive the radiance of your hope as this morning dawns tearless. There is a cross to bear, but when I gaze at you, I find the power to carry it. Life will win. Thank you and amen.

199.

Ah, Lord, there is no such thing as a small sorrow. If my heart sighs, your ears are ready to listen; if a worry enters my mind, however slight, you sympathetically bid me cast it upon you. You, who are familiar with the sorrows this life can hold, gladly walk with me through my small distresses; your love that bore the greatest sorrow will not begrudge carrying my small ones. Grant me the grace to carry my cross under the shadow of yours; let us weep together when we must, and then rejoice together through it all. Thank you and amen.

200.

Lord, I usually am confident of your eager mercy, but today, I am begging for it. I admit the ways I've acted are unbecoming: the thoughts that cast dark shadows on the landscape of my soul, unkindnesses, and impatience that lands on those near me. These realities rise up and accuse me. I admit to loving deeds I left undone. I am afraid I am a sham, offering praise and prayers while my soul feels flat and numb. Lord, I beg for your mercy; my sadness this day would shame me into retreating, but you invite, and I come, with head bowed and a slightly hopeful heart. I admit you are my loving savior. You hear my cry and welcome all of me. Thank you and amen.

201.

Lord, I stand on the threshold of a new season of my life. Let your words of peace welcome me into the unknown. I incline my ear to hear your voice. Quiet my fear, soothe my agitation, and strengthen my heart. Pausing in your presence, I rejoice, for you are present and faithful. I hear you say that you are with me—that I need not fear. That you are my help and need not dismay. That you will carry me when I grow weary. That you have called me and will stand by my side. To my poor and needy heart, you give revitalizing water; grace is offered to comfort my sorrow and correct my sin. Holy energy is mine when I grow faint and feeble. You will walk with me every step of this journey. I rest on your promise; I have nothing to fear. Thank you and amen.

202.

Oh, Unseen Love, whose depth and width I cannot comprehend, I see evidence of your beautiful light and my body longs for the rest only you can provide. Your voice invites me to trust your love and prove the lightness of your yoke, and I want to, yet my wayward heart often pulls me off course. As often as I stray, call me back. You have taught me that true peace is mine when I hide in you. Empty pastimes, earthly appetites vie with you to be my refuge, Lord; reign in my heart and rule all its movements. Oh Helping Love, grant me aid to take the narrow road, the one that leads to Abba's house. I hear you remind me, "I am your Love, your God, your All!" Thank you and amen.

203.

Great God, it is by your merciful hand that I rise this day; may gratitude for your kindness be my compass until this day closes. Both day and night, at home or away, may your vigilance hold me safe, your ceaseless bounty feed me, and your unfailing wisdom guide me. My history, with all its errors and its glories, is redeemed by your grace; my future, though unknown by me, must fit your purpose for my salvation and thereby bless my world. My mood changes from day to day—elation, depression, hope, fear—yet recalling your words of healing spoken over me, I find joy and rest. Whatever may come, by your grace, I will praise your name until death seals my lips and releases my true self to perfectly praise your goodness and glory. Thank you and amen.

204.

Lord, I am so weary of not feeling well. I have hints of healing, and then I'm back to the toilet or grimacing in pain or clenching my muscles. It's exhausting. You are familiar with discomfort, so I ask you to be with me as I bear it. Give me good cheer. I'll take what comes, for you are with me. But I confess, I feel like Elijah, I want to find a broom tree, lay down, and give up. Like him, I cry, "I have had enough." (1 Kings 19:4,5) I have fought the good fight, and now I am weary of the wounds. I would like to go to sleep and wake up when the healing is complete. I hear you whisper to me, "Come, weary one, I will give you rest." I lean upon your breast, and I am calmed. My foe is stern and eager for my defeat, but in my admitted weakness, you have made me strong. Hold me close, for I fear I'll faint. Thank you and amen.

205.

Oh my soul, continue to hang on to Christ, your strength, your life, your joy. By God's good grace, run straight into his arms. Keep looking into his face, so you do not get distracted and venture off the path. Cast your cares onto your Lord. Lean on him, and his mercy will be sufficient. Do not grow faint; do not fear. You are perfectly safe in his arms. He held you yesterday, and he will hold you tomorrow—he doesn't change. Remember, you are dear to his heart. Thank you and amen.

206.

The tempest raged fiercely over the sea. Your disciples watched its intensity increase with anxious hearts, while you slept soundly, calm, and still. They cried to you in their terror, "Save us, or we'll perish." (Mark 4:38,39) Your word rose above the noise of the vicious sea and declared, "Peace. Be still." Upon hearing your word, the wild winds quieted, the angry waves lowered, and the breakers ceased their pounding. So, Lord, when the sea within me rages, when fear squeezes my heart, when anxious thoughts storm my mind, let me hear your words, "Peace. Be Still." I will cling to these words until my soul is settled. Thank you and amen.

207.

Oh my soul, why do you cower; my heart, why do you wander? You can stand still and tall in the presence of the God who loves you. The kind and gentle shepherd gathers and protects you. His mercy is wide; his justice is freedom. Your sorrows are known in the heart of your savior, and your failings are forgotten. Ah, it is a great mercy to be forgiven. Greater still is the grace that releases your good. Jesus, complete your healing work in me, for your sorrow bought me joy. Oh, my soul, don't waste the Lord's goodness; don't make it more complicated than it is—God's love is offered, his kindness is rich, and his grace has the final say. Thank you and amen.

208.

Thank you, God, for all the bright, splendorous, noble beauty that fills the earth you created. Thank you, also, for the constant gifts of love that surround me. Even in dark moments, love can be found. And thank you that my joy is touched with pain, that shadows darken my lovely gardens, that my roses have thorns, for these imperfections remind me that earth's beauty is not the end. It reminds me of the perfection that will follow. Lord, I thank you for wisely giving me all I need, yet still leave me longing for more—more peace, joy, and rest. This more I yearn for is satisfied only when I lean upon your breast. Come let us be together. Thank you and amen.

209.

The manna fell each morning, enough for the day's need; oh my soul, pay attention, for the Lord's mercy continues to provide your daily bread. Promised strength is given to you for this day, even for this minute. Don't worry about the next day or even the next hour. Your God will grant you the grace to bear whatever it holds. Lord, my truest heart's prayer is thy will be done. Holy Spirit, align my mind, my emotions, and my body with my heart's cry. I hear you say to me, "Cast your cares on me, for I care for you. Trust me, and you will find joy and strength for the day." Thank you and amen.

210.

Spirit of Grace, Love Most Holy, ignite your fire within my heart. Replace my unnecessary fears with thoughts of your presence. Let love settle me. Speak to me of your pardoning grace; release me to live freely and joyfully. Precious Lamb of God, remove from me the stain of sin; seal my heart with the assurance of your delight. Grant me life and peace; seal my heart with the assurance of your power to save. Breathe on me, in me, and through me. May I rest upon you as I live this day. Keep me close, guard my way, fill me with joy, and never let me wander from your gaze. Thank you and amen.

211.

Oh, Jesus, you are my fastest friend. Your love has been the landscape of my life—always there, sometimes overlooked, yet when I notice its beauty, I am drawn to love you in return. You have bound me to your heart with cords of kindness and faithfulness that nothing can sever, for I am yours, and you are mine. Not only did you give your life for me, but also you also gave yourself to me! I return all I have and all I am to you. You are the source of my strength, the beating of my heart, and the breath of my life. I trust you to guard my way, to keep me safe wherever and through whatever the path leads. Your hand holds mine, and we walk life's road together. I am convinced that nothing can separate me from your love–not life nor death, not sickness nor health, not stress nor relief can pull my hand from yours. You hold me tight, and nothing can snatch me out of your grasp. Thank you and amen.

212.

Lord, I am weary of my humanity, its weaknesses in body and soul. I long for perfection, and I hear your voice bidding me toward it. Other voices, though, remind me of how short I fall of your glory. To whom shall I listen? The one who would pull me toward completion and joy or the one who would keep me stranded in shame and defeat? Your voice tells me to turn around, admit my faults, and walk in your freedom. Jesus, it is your voice I will heed, for it is your death that bought me life. It is your kindness that makes me a child of heaven, your grace that pardons, and your perfection that sets me free. Like the grateful tears of the prostitute proved her sins forgiven, may my life today prove your love at work within and through me. Thank you and amen.

213.

Lord, I am feeling low and a little depressed. The cancer is much smaller but still evident. The doctor says the radiation is still working. In six weeks, we'll have a better idea of where we stand. I am weary of it, want to be done with it, want to move on. But this is where we are today. Selah. So I welcome the sadness; I grieve for the wholeness my mind and body desires. I join you, Jesus, in the waiting and the gloom. I hear your words, "Watch and pray." (Matthew 26:41) The war is won, but the battle continues. I will gird myself with the armor of the Spirit and watch and pray. Thank you and amen.

214.

Lord, this day, walk beside me. Show me your face in the people I encounter, the tasks I undertake, and the tender beauty of the roses. Let your words bring me ease as I earnestly seek your face. Lord, you know all the cares that could weigh me down and the impatience and anger I have toward my bodily breakdowns. Apart from your uplifting grace, I could lose hope and fall victim to defeat. Strengthen my desire to follow you; illuminate and eliminate the subtle cares that would distract me from your will. Grant me the grace to choose life. I want to hear well done at the end of this day. Thank you and amen.

215.

I come with joy this morning to bring you my appreciation and to sing with all the saints my gratitude for your sustaining grace. It's true, I pass through the fire of affliction, yet your love walks with me, perfecting my wholeness. Your love, which claimed me as your own, will keep me as your own forever. May this magnetic love hold me true when the wind of fear attempts to blow me off course, when the attraction of passing pleasure entices me to take a shortcut, or when my resistance to obedience lulls me into mindlessness. I will keep in mind the restoration of my true self, which is the goal of your love for me, and choose life. Thank you and amen.

216.

Jesus, your voice beckons my laden heart. I respond, and your good word lightens my soul with the assurance of things I long to experience: freedom from guilt, unmerited favor, an undisturbed mind, joy overflowing, and unceasing love. Your voice beckons my wandering heart to allow you to direct my ways. I come, and your presence fills me with peace and confidence. I will heed your voice of love and trust my ways to your good will. Your voice beckons my exhausted body and to come and find energy. I trade my slacking best efforts for your excelling victory. Grant me might to continue to run the good race. I come, and you welcome me. I rest in your grace, I trust in your plan, and I live by your life. Thank you and amen.

217.

I put my trust in you, Lord Jesus, only you—trusting you for the gifts of your great love, for complete wholeness, and for healing. Your kind mercy reassembles the pieces of my broken body and soul; I trust you for the restoration of my true self. Father, your plan is for the ones you love to live this day as replicas of your son, so guide my steps, interactions, responses, and words. I will trust you for the power to be Jesus to my world. I put my trust in God's love, and God will supply all my needs. Thank you and amen. [A prayer based on Psalm 52]

218.

Lord, just as I trust in your work on the cross for my forgiveness, so I trust in your work of resurrection for my daily living. You are my plan and my power. Like you, I want to carry the cross this day brings, to help bear the burdens of my fellow sojourners, and to want only the Father's will. May grace expand and leave no room for selfishness. May kindness infuse my life's blood, and may peace filter the day's sorrows and joys. Love, conquer my darker moods. Mercy, be the oxygen I inhale. Forgiveness, be the breath I release. Thank you and amen.

219.

The hour may be dark, the temptation may be strong, but I need not fear, for Jesus is my light and my tower. Despair is not my lot, for the resurrection power of Christ sustains my hope. Though I experience physical distress and emotional hardship, my Lord, familiar with pain and sorrow, draws near, and I am comforted; he is my living bread, nourishing my body and soul. He will provide all I need. I am enveloped in his grace, and his goodness wraps me tight. When my prayers are faint and my love burns low, his intercession never ceases. Whatever may befall me, this I know for certain: Jesus is mine, and I am his. Thank you and amen.

220.

Holy is the Father. Holy is the Son. Holy is the Spirit. I wake with a song of awe in my heart for you, the beauty of all your creation, including humankind (even me). Your mercy astounds me. Your power quiets me. Your surrounding presence assures me. Thank you. You who are without beginning or end, receive the praise offered by the works of your hands—angels do your bidding with joy, humankind does their best to love as you have loved, and earth and creatures follow their assigned course. We live by faith, for though only the eyes of our hearts have beheld your face, we are convinced of your power (it saves me), of your love (it seeks me), and of your holiness (it convicts me). Today, may I walk in the path of your holiness. Thank you and amen.

221.

Oh, Loving God, who bends low to share my pain and sorrow, I cast my care on you. It feels like a long and weary journey, yet I don't fear the darkness or avoid the steepness since you walk it with me. Outside my window, the Rose of Sharon's returning blossom reminds me that you are faithful in all the seasons of my life. When suffering is my companion, you carry me in your arms; when pleasure accompanies my journey, you smile along with me. You are always near and forever dear. Thank you and amen.

222.

Dear one, your refuge is in the Lord, in God's holy temple, and in his holy space. The help you need to bear this load is not found in demanding answers, whirring thoughts, ceaseless questions, and chasing experts. These quests and questions only serve to grab and pull you away from the one place you can find peace and gain some clarity. You understand this, but how do you get to the quiet of refuge when the tempest of worry and fear beats upon your mind and heart? Remember God sees all. God is not off duty; God has not abandoned you and your loved ones. Let your doubts crash upon the solid foundation of God's proven love. Your doubts will crumble, and quiet will rise from the dust.

> I've already run for dear life
> straight to the arms of God.
> So why would I run away now
> when you say,
> "Run to the mountains; the evil
> bows are bent, the wicked arrows
> Aimed to shoot under cover of darkness
> at every heart open to God.
> The bottom's dropped out of the country;
> good people don't have a chance"?
> But God hasn't moved to the mountains;
> his holy address hasn't changed.
> He's in charge, as always, his eyes
> taking everything in, his eyelids
> Unblinking, examining Adam's unruly brood
> inside and out, not missing a thing.
> God's business is putting things right;
> he loves getting the lines straight,
> Setting us straight. Once we're standing tall,
> we can look him straight in the eye.
> Psalm 11 (MSG)

223.

I am held safe in the arms of Jesus. I rest in his gentle embrace; his love is the blanket that warms me. In this close embrace, I can more easily hear him whisper words of comfort, murmurings of hope, assurances of love. In the closely held arms of Jesus, I am safe from the corrosive nature of worry. No real harm can reach me when his arms hold me tight. Sorrow causes me to cling to him. Fear moves me to bury my head in his chest. Jesus, my refuge, my rock, I will remain in your arms. Hold me tight this day. Thank you and amen.

224.

Jesus, your love for me is so profound, my mind cannot totally grasp it, and my words fall short of describing it. Yet I understand enough to be forever thankful for it. Knit my heart to yours, and in it let nothing rival you for my affection and my allegiance. Fill me with your love, expand it to the farthest reaches and deepest fissures of my soul, so that there is no room for impatience, indifference, and ill-will. Train my every thought, word, and act according to your love. Oh Light of Love, may your healing beam melt away all diseases, cares, worries, and sorrows. When suffering comes, be my peace. In weakness, be my power. When storms blow, be my refuge. I rest in you until I wake in you. Thank you and amen.

225.

Lord, I have the assurance that you are leading me. What more can I ask? There is no denying your faithful mercy given me in the past; even today, I experience your peace and hear your word beckon me to dwell in you. My response: I trust you, Lord, whatever befalls me, for I know you work all things for good. You accompany me on this journey, cheering each of my faltering steps, granting me grace for each trial, nourishing me through the kindness of the saints. Joy leads me homeward where my Father is running toward me. Thank you and amen.

226.

Oh, Lamb of God, in my sickness, hold me close to your wounded side; hidden in your suffering, I find peace and perspective. The clutch of death harries me. The fear of failure in remaining faithful teases me. Only your seeking and finding grace holds me still. As I abide in you, my life is secure, conflicts diminish, and love ascends. I know only a small portion of your face, but it is beautiful enough to sustain and hold me true. Smile on me, Lamb of God. Thank you and amen.

227.

Lord, I am afraid. I fear the return of the sharp pain. When my mind runs ahead, anticipating discomfort, hold me in the present, breathe with me in the now. The pain proves my body is changing and something is happening. May I bravely endure the pain that comes with eliminating the death within me. When your sojourning people were small in number and of no account, you would not let the ravaging kings touch or harm them; I bear the same description and beg the same protection. As it was with them, may it be with me. Bring me out of the darkness with joy and singing. Praise the Lord! Thank you and amen.

228.

My inner ear hears the name of Jesus, and my sorrows are soothed, my wounds are quieted, and my fear is held at bay. In Jesus' name, my spirit is secure, and my body, though still teased by pain, rests in peace. Abounding grace fills the storehouse of my soul and is the shield that protects me. Jesus, lead me, dear shepherd; befriend me, dear companion; love me, dear spouse. Speak words of hope, of unity, and of a good future, for you are my source and my goal. Accept my imperfect praise, and through me, show yourself glorious. Thank you and amen.

229.

"Be of good cheer, your sins are forgiven." (Matthew 9:2) His body was broken. That was obvious since he needed to be carried into your presence on a pallet by his four friends. Less obvious, but more importantly, his heart was broken. You knew he needed the comfort of forgiveness more than the restoration of his mobility. Like the paralytic, my body is broken. Discouraged by the ravaging symptoms of my cancer treatment, I complain of discomfort and the insistent demands of my bowels. I am weary of the fatigue and of the caution I must practice ("don't overdo it," "stay out of the sun," and so on). Jesus, you see my discouragement about my physical limitations, but first, you speak to my heart about its need for forgiveness. You gently point out that my discouragement is a product of sin. Impatience lurks within it. You reveal a part of me that expects health, that compares the state of my body today to what it was six months ago and comes up disappointed. My heart very subtly lives in discontentment, and I am robbed of your joy. You see my heart and touch it with kindness. You remind me that I am not in control and that you are always good and will bring good. My spirit calms, and I am content to trust you. [A prayer based on Matthew 9:1-8]

I keep the Lord always before me;
because he is at my right hand, I shall not be moved.
Therefore my heart is glad, and my soul rejoices;
my body also rests secure.
For you do not give me up to Sheol
or let your faithful one see the pit.
You show me the path of life.
In your presence, there is fullness of joy;
in your right hand are pleasures forevermore.
[A prayer based on Psalm 16:8-11]

Addendum to this morning's prayer: Dear friends, I want to make myself clear. I believe my complaints are legitimate; my desire for healing and wholeness align with God's desire for me, and my cries for deliverance are welcomed by the God who loves me. But the pit into which I can fall is to focus on my sufferings, to let them capture my attention and let them be what defines me. When I allow my sufferings to consume my mind and heart, there is little room for the presence of God. When I fill my mind with the promises and presence of God, I can settle in peace—a much better space than angst and discontent for healing to be realized.

230.

God says to me, "Quiet down, hold your body still, turn off the patter in your head, breathe, open your heart to my ministrations, and you will be convinced that I am God." Thank you and amen.

231.

How precious it is when we live together in peace. Father God, loving you and being loved by you fills my heart to overflowing with goodwill toward others; it also delights you and fulfills your command. Tenderize my heart, so I feel the sighs of my friends and share in their joy. Eliminate the envy and scorn residing in my heart, for they block love. Instead, grant me a covering grace that sees the good in others and forgives the bad. When we gather, may it be a sweet reunion ruled by love. It is the bond that holds us together and joins us with you. Thank you and amen.

232.

As I read Psalm 81, joy sets the stage. In the celebration, I hear your voice saying to me, "You are free now. I lifted the burden that weighed you down. I took from your hands the load you carried. I heard your distress and saved you. You may not have recognized me. I was camouflaged in what seemed a storm, and that place where it seemed you were without resource is where I perfected your strength and trust. Pay attention! In the storms and the apparent lack is where you will find the idols you worship, the things you look to for comfort, peace, provision. Won't you voluntarily strip yourself of these alien gods? I am your God. I'm the source of freedom and provision. Trust me, and I will satisfy all your needs. Or don't. Continue in your stubborn ways and remain angry. It's your choice. But choose life, won't you?" Father, there are places of disobedience to which I have run, trying to hide from your face, foolishly squandering your grace. But your voice reaches me in my lonely corner, and aware of how I've cooperated with death, I return to you with embarrassment and hope. I see you coming to meet me, rejoicing in my return, carrying the gifts of my inheritance. You are Lord, lover of those who banish themselves from your presence, as well as those who seek it. You are always compassionate, forgiving, and tender. May I respond to your kindness by faithfully returning to your faithfulness. I receive your blessing, your pardon, and your peace. Thank you and amen.

233.

Nature is an open book. Every page declares praise for her creator God. But greater praise is due to God for the grace that rescued humankind, written with the ink of Christ's precious blood. The cross is the penultimate chapter of God's book of love. In it, the power, the wisdom, and the love of the author are detailed. Oh, the bittersweet wonder of the cross, where love and death compete. Love wins, though the cost is great: profound wounds and a bleeding side. The final chapter has begun; songs of praise unending, the Kingdom come and coming, the Lamb victorious on the throne, and all creation loved and loving. Thank you and amen.

234.

Oh, Christ, my king, you've given gifts that are mine through all eternity, you've given works of wonder that inspire me to sing your praise, and when I focus on your great love, my heart fills with thanks and worry has no room. I thank you for the saints who have gone before me, leaving footprints to mark the way: patriarchs and apostles, desert abbas and ammas, Mother Teresa and Billy Graham. They teach me to yearn for you, to hold hope, to lift my head and be done with shame, to trust your overcoming power. Let your love strengthen me so that my life is a signpost that points to you, so that my weakness proves your power, and so that my shared gifts are evidence of your grace. Thank you and amen.

235.

The good news of Easter continues; rest, my soul, the fight is over: Jesus has triumphed! Praise you, Jesus. The enemy did his best, but he has been defeated; your life causes the shadow of death to melt away. Walk now with confidence and joy into the dawn of this new day! Thank you and amen.

236.

Always living, forever creating, maker of all things, you are the ruler of the day and the night; you give sleep to refresh our bodies and morning light to stir our spirits. Darkness flees as the morning star appears. I hear the crow of my neighbor's rooster, awakening me to a day held by your grace. Peter heard the same sound and cried tears of shame and repentance. At the break of this day, like Peter, I know my faltering heart, and I seek your face. Held in your gaze, I am free from the faults that cling, and I can walk into the day with you as my guide, my power, my companion, and my joy. Thank you and amen.

237.

Lord, there are some mornings when I feel as foggy in my head as it is outside my window. Today is one of them. I woke thirsty and shuffled to the kitchen for a drink of water, wanting but unable to go back to sleep. Instead, I sit to pray. Lord, train my soul to thirst for you, as I thirst for a drink of water in the night. Come, Spirit of God, wrap me in your presence as the dew gently blankets the grass; fall on the parched places of my soul as a welcomed shower on a desert plane. As the dry earth cracks open because it needs rain, my soul breaks open for want of you. The sun just broke through the fog, and your Spirit shines light into the darkness of my spirit. It is for you I thirst, and my hope will not be disappointed. Thank you and amen.

238.

Jesus, you promised to those who follow you that where you are, we shall also be. I go with you today—my master, who deserves my obedience, and my friend, who desires my loyalty. Jesus, by your strength, I promise to follow where you lead. Grant me the grace to keep my word. You left footprints to mark the way I should walk. Guide me into love, call me into service, and draw me close to your heart. When I falter, you will catch and uphold me. Savior and friend, walk with me as I earnestly stumble toward heaven. Thank you and amen.

239.

Lord Jesus, you are the living Word, and you embody every truth and every promise preserved in the Holy Scriptures. We look to the written word to show us your face. Holy Spirit, you inspired the authors, and you illuminate my understanding when I read the law and the prophets. Heavenly Father, each morning I open your word to hear your voice of love, and you never fail. I listen and learn of my true self, formed after your image; my false self, broken by sin and passing away; my vocation, to receive and then give away your love. Your glory shouts from the word, your faithfulness whispers; your mercy is the constant melody hummed from Genesis to Revelation. Attune my heart to your song of salvation, and give me words to share your profound and simple love to the world around me. Thank you and amen.

240.

Holy love, outpacing all other loves—come, bring your joy, and make your home in my heart. Jesus, you are the compassionate one, source of unfettered love. Shower my fearful heart with your saving grace. Loving Spirit, breathe peace into my heart! May I enter into your promised rest. Woo me so that sin has no pull on my soul; be to me my beginning and end, and set me free. Thank you and amen.

241.

Arms extended, hands open wide, it was not with money that you paid the debt of humankind. As I reach for your hands, grab mine and hold me forever. Let the power of your blood strengthen my weak heart. Arms wide open, ready to embrace the whole of broken humanity, carry me to love and perfect rest. Lord, it saddens me that my return of love is so poor, yet your grace is rich. I seek your face, and joy replaces sadness. My mind and heart see through the cross to your throne. Your hands are still reaching, ready to receive my all. My living is for your glory, my dying is for love of you. Thank you and amen.

242.

Jesus, you are the true longing of my heart; your gift to me is freedom and release from my fears and my sins. In you, I find rest and consolation. You are the world's hope if only we would turn to you. For you were born to deliver us into the Kingdom of your Father; when you reign, grace and glory abound. By your merit, raise us to our best selves. Thank you and amen.

243.

The scripture says you will come to judge the world. I say, "Come quickly; the sooner the better." With your judgment, lies will be exposed and fall away. Truth will stand unhindered. Yes, come quickly, for worry and fear cannot exist when you are near. Come quickly, bring your Kingdom and authority to all the earth and within my life. For with your reign, sin loses its pull, and pain and sorrow subside. Yes, come quickly, for your rule is the only hope of peace for this broken and dismembered world. Come quickly, come today. Thank you and amen.

244.

My dear God, your creation, earth and human alike, ache for fear to cease and your peace to reign; for things that unite humankind to be honored more than the things that divide; for your justice, not earthly might to be what guides our decisions. Come Holy Spirit, come, Prince of Peace, come, Father of all creation. Come. Thank you and amen.

245.

Open your eyes, look around, see the glory of the Lord coming toward you. His anger is aroused because of wickedness and lies. He will not let evil prevail. His truth will prove more powerful than fear. He calls for all humankind to stand before his throne and sifts out pride and greed. Why wouldn't I rush to him for such an accounting? Oh, Jesus, expose me to your glory, change the shape of my heart. As Julia Ward Howe said in "The Battle Hymn of Republic": "You died to make men holy. Let me live to make all free." In the name of the Father, the Son, and Holy Spirit. Thank you and amen.

246.

Lord, I join with all your people praying for your healing to come to the world. Awake in us just and generous spirits that share of the abundance you have given. A life marked by love is our hope and our goal. Lord, walk with us from despair into freedom. Let war and hatred end so that we can know peace. I will act toward others as you have acted toward me with goodness and kindness; I pray such love shown will diminish their fears and increase their peace. Lord, do away with all that kills abundant living, pride that separates, teachings that do not breathe, disrespect for all life. Lord, you have made us in your image. Dust away the grime that hides the beauty of our lives. Thank you and amen.

247.

Jesus, your glory fills the sky with your light and truth. Rise in me like the sun in the East. Chase away the shades of night. For this morning, I am grumpy and cheerless. Your mercy is what I need to return me to joy. Shine within me; make me glad and tender. Come, visit my soul. Break through the numbness and apathy; source of life, pour into me your energy, wash away my gloom. Grant me the grace to see your beauty and your perfection this morning, to hear your voice of love. Then speak it to my world. Thank you and amen.

248.

I come face to face with my resistance to love when I sit still with you, Lord; my demands, resentments, detachment, and pride all rise to the surface. Skim them from me as cream from the milk. You have every reason to remove me from your presence because all these sins grieve you. But hear my plea. Return me to the place where my joy lives. Animate me with your powerful Spirit. From this vantage point, I will have something to say to those tempted to turn away from life. They will hear your voice of love and return to you. I trust you; do your good will in me, rebuild a community that will surround me. Life works better when such boundaries exist. Thank you and amen. [A prayer based on Psalm 51:3,4,12,13,18,19]

249.

Let musical instruments release their songs today, let human voices join the chorus of praise to God for saints who have left a model to follow. St. Cecelia, the patron of music, devoted to and trusted God with her very person. Let me also trust you and raise my voice in prayer. Thank you and amen.

250.

I come to you a thankful soul, grateful for the ways you've allowed me to work and have provided for me and my loved ones. This morning the storm rages, the snow falls, the wind blows, but we are safe. We have what we need, and now I come before you to say thanks. All the earth is your garden, including humankind. I bring you my flowers of praise. Deal with the weeds that choke the flowers. Make me a beautiful garden, oh gardener of my soul. You shall eliminate all the weeds one day, and I will know the joy of purity. Oh, Lord, let this day come quickly and let it begin now; free me from sorrow and sin. I dwell in your presence and sing your praise. Thank you and amen.

251.

One of the most beautiful things I can undertake is to give you thanks, oh Lord. So I do—praise to you, Lord Jesus Christ, King of endless glory. The morning sheds light on your faithful kindness. Your favor awaits me at each turn of the hour. The singing birds announce a new day, new mercy. Oh Lord, you have made my heart glad. You are working a deep wonder in my body and a renewed hope in my soul. May I live in the triumph of this new day. Thank you and amen.

252.

Oh, dear Jesus, my soul is cushioned by your care for me at this moment. I look at you walking on the road to Emmaus, speaking tender words of instruction to your friends, and I find my own heart warming within me. I have the strength to return to Jerusalem. I feel the shroud of shame lifting from my heart, and I can see your glory leading me toward life in union with your will. Grant me a day of unsullied devotion to you, a day where praise of you is my language, a day that is a shadow of the eternal day where burdens are banned and rest is the work given me to do. Thank you and amen.

253.

Complete confidence is mine, for I belong to Jesus and he to me; the joy I have is just a hint of the glory I will experience in heaven. Count the blessings: I am born into life, God has chosen me, and the Holy Spirit empowers me with Jesus' great love and sacrifice so that I can walk shamelessly. Living for your will makes me completely happy. I see the beauty of heaven. I hear the shouts of mercy and the tender murmurs of love. I can rest when I walk with you, content yet eager for more union. Gazing upon you fills me with acts of goodness. Your love is the only destination I choose. You fill my heart with song, and praising you is my greatest goal throughout my day. Thank you and amen.

254.

As much as my friends would like to, they cannot love me perfectly. Only you can, Jesus. Doubts and fear come toward me as quickly as the future. Jesus, stop their assault. Stand between me and the storm. I declare that you alone are the only one who will never let me down. Thank you and amen.

255.

Oh Lord, the safest place I can put myself is at the foot of your cross. It is here I want to make my home. It is here I find rest and relief. When I recall the price you paid, I am moved to sorrow over my brokenness, which necessitated your death, and awed at the love you hold for me, which made you willing to suffer on my behalf. It makes no sense, I know, but in the shadow of your cross is where light dwells—light that makes choices clearer and gratefulness abound, where the radiance of your glory overcomes my sinful self. Thank you and amen.

256.

Lord, despair knocks on the door. I arm myself with remembering your call to me and your cross-proved mercy toward me. I pause before I answer the knock and attend to the spark of holy love you've placed within me. Selah. Courage to turn away despair arises when I remember who you are: God of glory, Son of humility, Spirit of hope. Praising you energizes me. I can open the door. Despair, like a doormat, serves to ready me for your presence. Thank you and amen.

257.

Lord, God, you sent John, the baptizer, to ready the world for your coming. His voice still cries out from the desert, urging me to follow God's ways—to turn from my precious sins and submerge myself in the living water that cleanses my heart, my thoughts, and my will, to let the Lord who loves me control my life. He pleads for me to forsake my own agenda and to pursue the life of the Kingdom: one marked by justice, truth, and love. These are the filters through which I decide what to think, say, and do. Anything not rooted in these is not to be trusted. Oh, Lamb of God, I look to you. Send your power, send your hope, let me see your face. Thank you and amen.

258.

Jesus, my creator, sustainer of all nature, your fingerprints are on all creation. I find hints of your involvement in all I see. The bare winter trees stripped of their lush leaves express your humble humanity. The orange glow on the horizon promises a rising sun and light to live by. My dogs, Pepper and Ellie, trust me just as you trusted your Father. Thank you for the evidence displayed all around me of your care and love. You formed this earth and suffered upon it saving humankind. Angels, glorious beings, Jesus, whom you praise day and night, chose to dwell among us. He became like me so that I could become like him. Vast and unending space, you are confined within his being. This creator and container knew the confinement of a manger and a cross. Thank you and amen.

259.

Jesus, you stood on the mountain, and for a moment, your divinity shone through. You dazzled and blazed. I dare a glimpse, and I praise you. The prophets and the law join in the praise; the clouds cover, and God's voice announces your truth: beloved, pleasing Son. A word was given to me, "Listen to him." (Mark 9:7) I will. Speak, oh loved Jesus. I listen and adore you. Thank you and amen.

260.

Dear Lord, just as you broke the loaves beside the sea of Galilee, feeding the crowds, would you break open the bread of your word and feed me this morning? I seek you beyond the pages of scripture. Your words are the door I walk through to meet you. I am waiting for your presence. Break the chains that keep me captive, the habits that bind me to death so that peace, not frantic hoarding, rules my days. You are the food of my life. Your word rescues me. Your love teaches me to love. Send your Spirit today to open my eyes to see your face through the scriptures, through my writings, through my encounters. Come, walk with me. Thank you and amen.

261.

With your strength, oh Christ, I will fight for the good life, the Kingdom life; now and throughout eternity, it is my joy and crown. With my eyes fixed on you, oh Christ, I will run the race; you are the path and the prize. Worries will not hinder me, for I depend upon your generous mercy to provide. Trust proves that you are my life and my love. Oh, my soul, do not grow weary, do not fear. God holds you close; you are important to your Lord. Christ, you are my all. Thank you and amen.

262.

Dear Lord, I read in the gospels of the great crowds that gathered around you, eager to hear your teaching and experience your power. Today, in the gospel of my life, I, too, draw near you, eager for your gracious smile and tender touch. You have said the well do not need a physician, but I need you. There are many sin-sick regions of my soul that if left unabated spread the cancer of apathy, the polio of despair, the leprosy of indifference. I come and touch the hem of your garment. Send your power to heal me. Do not delay. Show me your salvation now. I kneel in hope and rise in power. Praise you, great Physician. Thank you and amen.

263.

God, you cry out to your people and me, begging us to come to you, reminding us that you long to comfort us and that your peace awaits us. You call us out of the darkness—to leave behind the weight of sorrow. You remind us that our sins are dealt with and done and that you share your victory with us. I heed your message. I will turn around and walk toward your Kingdom. Come to me, Holy Spirit, help me clear away the debris littering the path that leads to my heart. Let's knock down the barricades that block our joining. I long to welcome you as you welcome me. I've taken the long way home for too long. It is time to get on the highway that takes me directly to your heart. Send out a work crew to fill in the potholes that slow my journey to your Kingdom. My life is yours to rule. I gladly rely on you. You will keep your promises. Thank you and amen.

264.

Come, Lord. Come. Befriend my heart. Enter the ache of my body. I know and take comfort in the end of the story, your victorious defeat of death and the entering of your eternal throne room. But I am in the midst of the strife. My body and soul feel like a crumpled piece of aluminum foil formed into a tightly wadded ball. I long for the ease of stretching out and breathing deeply. I think of you, stretched out upon the cross, each breath you took a battle. Lord of the cross, gently stretch me. Match my breath to yours. I am not alone in this conflict. In it, I join myself to you and find strength. Thank you and amen.

265.

Lord, look upon our broken world; it seems unrest and greed are on the increase. Somehow, grant your peace to yearning hearts. We yearn for a world where guns are laid down, and bombs are dismantled, a world where peace is our rule. O Jesus, you are the Prince of Peace. It is only by your grace that this dream can be realized. Peace, be my guide. In Advent, we anticipate the celebration of your birth. Begin now, be born in me today. I choose to practice peace, peace within my heart, between friends, and even toward my enemies. Come Holy Spirit. Thank you and amen.

266.

Forever Father, strong to save, able to calm the raging sea and limit the approach of the ocean's waves, hear me as I pray for the ones I love tossed about by trouble. Saving Jesus, whose voice ruled the wind and waves, whose feet trod the sea as if it were solid ground, who slept unaffected by the storm, hear me as I pray for the ones I love tossed about by trouble. Hovering Spirit, who spoke order out of chaos and instituted peace out of confusion, hear me as I pray for the ones I love tossed about by trouble. Loving and powerful Trinity, shield me from danger of every kind. Go with me as my protector and friend. You have my praise in both trouble and security. Thank you and amen.

267.

A paraphrase of the hymn "Be Still my Soul" by Jean Sibelius: Oh my soul, rest: the Lord is with you. Hold up under sorrow and pain. God has not forgotten you. Your situation changes, but God does not; the God who guided and provided for you yesterday will do the same today. Oh my soul, rest: Jesus is your best friend. He will lead you to joy. Right now, God is actively preparing a good life for you. Don't waver in your trust; soon all will be as clear as day. Rest, my soul: the storm stirring in you will obey his voice just as the wind did over Galilee. Oh my soul, rest: time passes so quickly. Soon the day will come when you shall see Jesus face to face; all disappointments, fears, losses will be gone, and only love, pure love will remain. Come quickly, Lord Jesus. Let me taste this feast today. Thank you and amen.

268.

Dear Lord and Creator of all humankind, forgive me my foolish ways, rewire my mind to think as you do, purify my acts of service, deepen my sense of awe. Let my trust be simple, like the fisherman who heard your call; let me leave all and follow you. I will rest as Jesus did, sharing my quiet with you, hearing your voice of love. Deepen my stillness. Layer by layer, remove the noise and clatter. Increase your peace within my heart so that my life reflects your beauty. As I try to quiet my mind and soul, desires flare. Cool them down with your breath of life, squelch their demands so that I can hear your still, small voice. Thank you and amen.

269.

God, you are a place where protection is sure, where defense never fails. When my human ails and woes threaten to overtake me, you are my helper. The enemy of my soul is strong and intends my harm; unhelped I would surely fall victim to his schemes, but you stand beside me, and you are stronger than he. The battle continues, but I am not afraid, for I know his end and the one who ends him: Jesus, the Christ. With a word, the enemy falls, and that victory triumphs through me. The Holy Spirit and her gifts are mine. All else is an added bonus. I am a citizen of God's enduring Kingdom. Thank you and amen.

270.

Lord, by your gift, I am a woman of promise, a container of hope. Fill me with your precious living water and let your goodness pour out through my words and speech. Lord, your ancient wisdom resides within my heart. I tend its flame. Its light reveals your presence and your plan. Your word is a lamp unto my feet. Lord, you are the dawn of justice. I reflect your character and share light with those who live in the shadows. Lord, your compassionate heart breaks over the world's pain. Break my heart; make it new so I can draw near and offer love to those who live in sorrow. Lord, I am a gospel account. I tell the good news through my life; I am a broken but beautiful home for the Lord of life. Thank you and amen.

271.

This morning, I read Psalm 81 and hear you say to me, "Stand still while I chew you out. You need to hear this, really hear this. I read you the riot act for a very good reason. DON'T DEPEND ON ANY GOD BUT ME. I am the one who miraculously carried you through the terrible times of your life. All you need to do is trust me. Demonstrate your trust, and I will take care of you. Open your mouth, and I will feed you and supply words to share. I said this to Israel all those years ago, and she wouldn't listen. She was done with me. So I let her go, let her seek her own welfare. Dear one, please, listen to me, walk in my ways. I will take care of the situations that threaten you. I will keep you safe." Thank you and amen.

272.

The transgressions I know about are always in my face, taunting me, shaming me, threatening to expose me as a fraud to the people around me. Still, the reality is that you are the one who matters in my world. My sin offends you, and it comes as no surprise to you. There is no denying I have failed, turned away from your path of life. I deserve your disapproval. Some of my favorite sins have been around for as long as I can remember. But I beg you, teach me wisdom from the inside out. I want my primary mode of operation to be truth. Lord, I tire of the long face attitude that sin leaves me with. Take me back to the place where my countenance lights with joy because of your mercy and love. I'll have something to say to my friends then, won't I? They'll want in on the connection with you! Lord, I need you to hold me back from shedding my sister's blood with my tongue, impatiently talking about her, demeaning her. Instead, let my tongue sing of your kindness and how great you are to save. Lord, my Lenten fast is offered out of love, not ritual nor expectation. You receive me with delight. Thank you and amen. [A prayer based on Psalm 51:3-6,12-14, 17]

273.

My enemies and foes are within me, taunting me, ganging up on me. Whispering, they seek to undermine my trust in you. Lord, it is true. I am not perfect; nothing I do comes from the purest motive, but I don't want to do nothing because my distrust of myself is greater than my trust in you. Let me act, trusting you to do the work of cleansing. Use my best efforts (tainted as they are) to bring about your Kingdom. Loving God, grant me a generous spirit, one that makes room for the outcasts, the lonely. Let me work for your Kingdom with a heart fueled by love. I dedicate my efforts to you, imperfect though they are. Receive them as I intend them, an offering of love. Increase my love; let it consume my mind and my actions. I remember the widows and orphans, the oppressed, and the victims. May I work toward justice grounded in love. Thy Kingdom come. Thank you and amen.

274.

There was only the hope of a God who cared at one time. My heart knew it was made for more. Then there was Jesus, whose beauty marred by sorrow ripped the veil, uniting me with the source of love. Hope is realized in you, Jesus. You reveal the face of God through your sorrow and your victory. Now you look on me with hope; you talk with your Father about me, speak of your plans for me, send your Spirit on assignment to aid and protect me. Oh, beloved one, thank you and praise you today and every day. Thank you and amen.

275.

The lamb upon the throne is worthy of every praise I can offer, every credit I can bestow, and everything valuable I own. When I truly listen, his anthem alone rings clear; all other songs quiet but the ones that come from him to the world. The crash of the wave, the steps of the servant, the laughter of the father—all are songs from his heart. Wake up, open yourself to the only song worth singing, the one that tells of the wonder of his saving love and declares your allegiance to him forever. I agree you are the Lord of Life. You conquered death and gladly share your victory over the strife of death with me. I will tell your story. You came to die. You died to live again. You live to grant me eternal life. Death has died! Oh Lord, your love was tested on the cross. I remember the wounds on your hands and side, wounds transformed into healing. Your love is mystery unfathomable, brightest gleam unbearable. I take great comfort in remembering you are the Lord of time. As I age and lose youth's assumed agility and freshness, I trust that you are my companion in the daily dying I wake to each morning. You hold the ages. You hold me. I shall praise you now and forever. Thank you and amen.

276.

Come to me, oh perfect love, find my longing heart and share your intense love with me. Come close, Comforting Spirit, ignite within my heart a fire that burns away my selfishness, that clothes me with power and illumines my path. I am restless until I find a resting spot for your Spirit to dwell. Great King of my heart, give me a song to sing, one that is worthy of your kindness. Glorious Father, victor over all forms of death, come rule over me, you whose wisdom has no beginning or end. Come beside me, God-made-flesh, be my defender. I have my eyes and my heart fixed on you, Jesus, God of wonder, help me live well today. Holy Comforter, bring to my mind the words of Jesus and the life and power of Jesus; live and pray within me. My one hope is to praise you today and every day into eternity. Thank you and amen.

277.

Your love, so vast, runs ahead of gale-force winds; it reaches every compass point on earth, fills the emptiness of space with your presence. Your love finds me. The sun illuminates your love, and the night cannot hide it. Your love, so great, stretches across time, unbeginning and unending—it encompasses human need. The sinner finds your love waiting when they quit running; it guides the lost one home. It is impossible to reach the end of your grace. Thank you and amen.

278.

I am firmly held in your love. You will not let me go. On such assurance, I can rest my weary soul. My life is yours; bathe it in your ocean of love so I can more richly experience your grace. Your great light surrounds me, and your blazing fire renews my flickering candle. Shine forth in and through me. This day, may I burn brightly and lovely. Your joy pursues me through grief and pain. How can I resist your invitation? I trust your promise of joy in the morning. Grant me the grace to bear the cross that today will bring. My daily deaths lead to eternal life. Thank you and amen.

279.

I sing your praise; you reign forever, creator of all, God of power, of love, and of my salvation. As I praise you, my soul is soothed with a healing balm, and doubt quiets its voice. Your presence draws close, bearing my sorrows—always present, always helping, granting peace, joy, and blessing. You gently lead me in the way I should go, thank you. Grant me the grace to follow. The way becomes less troubled when I keep my heart fixed on you. I offer songs of thanksgiving. May the world hear of your goodness through my joyful praise. I bear your name, and I give you glory. I know your power, and my life displays your wonder. I worship only you; all idols must fall because you alone are Lord and worthy of my praise. Thank you and amen.

280.

I nadequate as it is, I will raise my voice and sing praise to Jesus, the one who purchased me from death. I will speak of my rich and generous God and King. Lord, grant me the grace to form words that amply express your great name. Jesus, your presence calms my fear, quiets my sorrow. You are my favorite song. Each stanza describes the life, health, and peace you offer. You not only cancel the debt I owe because of my sin, but also you break its power over me in my daily life. Freedom is mine! To God, I give all glory, to Christ, all honor, to the Spirit, all thanks. Thank you and amen.

281.

My hope's foundation is the sacrificial love and generous righteousness of Jesus. On this, I build my life. All other grounds upon which I might choose to build my hope will ultimately fail me. I trust Jesus. Even when it seems he is absent and I can't find his face, his grace has trained me to trust. Because he is present, the storm may rage, but my anchor is secured within his heart of love. I am perfectly safe. One day he will bring me home. May I live this day in such a way as to better prepare me for the weight of glory he's preparing me. Today, I put on his righteousness and his character. Thank you and amen.

282.

Loving Lord, creating God, I stand in awe of the works of your hands, the rising sun spreading light across our world, the crash of thunder during yesterday's storm. All of nature reveals your greatness and calls forth a song of praise from me. It is beyond my comprehension that to free me from my sins, you, source and sustainer of creation, submitted to the cross and bled and died. I eagerly await the day when you will come and take me home. At that time, I will truly and completely offer you the praise and thanks you deserve. But for now, receive my praises and gratitude, as imperfect as they are. Thank you and amen.

283.

We are weary of heart, weary of doing good, especially those of us enduring the wreck of recent tragedies. We come to you just as we are: weary, worn, and sad. Grant us a restoring rest so we can continue our work. We are thirsty for life. Our souls need revival, especially those of us attempting to say no to addictions. We come to you just as we are: thirsty, hungry, and numb. Grant us a drink of the living water that quenches our true thirst. We doubt the light; we fear the future, especially as we hear the news of our country and our world. We come to you just as we are: doubting, worried, and afraid. Grant us hope in you, the light of the world, our morning star, and rising sun. Let us walk in the hope of your goodness, life, and light today. Thank you and amen.

284.

Oh Lord, when I consider what it cost you to bring me home, the cross upon which you died, I realize the emptiness of my precious possessions and the ridiculousness of my pride. You died, and I live. You are my most valued person; all other claims on my life must submit to your love. I look upon you on the cross and see your sorrow and love flowing out through the blood dripping from your hands and feet. They meant to mock you when they placed a thorny crown upon your head; instead, that crown perfectly names you as King, validated through your suffering. In response to such amazing love, I offer you my all. Thank you and amen.

285.

I come upon a fountain in a lovely garden. I expect sparkling water to flow from it; instead, I am surprised to find it filled with blood. It is your blood, the blood of the God who took on human flesh, and I know that it is the source of forgiveness. Blood is such an ugly image, but it was required for atonement. It represents your death and the work your death accomplished. The sinner crucified with you was the first to receive the gift of your death. Along with him, I ask you to remember me. Re-member me. Put me back together, make me whole. Wash off the stain of sin. The power of your death empowers your beloved to say no to the daily death invitations and habits I encounter. Your love is the subject of my life's song; I will sing it until I die, and after that, I will sing it perfectly. Thank you and amen.

286.

Lord, I watch with you at Gethsemane. I witness your torment and consider it a miracle that you could remain still. The evil one tempting you, yet again. Your sweat, your tears, your conflict, and then your resolve. Lord, teach me to pray. I sneak into the room and hear the accusations thrown at you and your silence in response. I cry when they mock and beat you; you catch my eye, and I grow calm. Lord, teach me to suffer. I follow you to the hill, where you are lifted onto the cross. I stay near and hear your labored breath. Your obedience finishes the work. Lord, teach me to die. I rush to the tomb to tend your lifeless body. I am heavy with grief, but where are you? You greet me by my name—you are alive! Lord, teach me to rise. Thank you and amen.

287.

Jesus, just bringing your name and your character to my mind brings me joy. I remember your saving love that bought my freedom, your death that is my ticket into God's forever presence. I love how I can count on you to be with me in my sorrow or distress, how you enter it and carry it with me. I love you because you loved me first. Thank you and amen.

288.

I call you Love. Oh, Love, deeper than the sea, broader than the heavens, higher than the stars, it is beyond my thoughts and imaginings that the God of Love took on our form for our sake! For us, he was baptized, bore the desert temptations, and overthrew the tempter. For us, he prayed, for us, he taught, for us, he worked wonders. He came seeking us, not himself. For us, he was betrayed, tortured, and crucified. For us, he gave his dying breath. For us, he rose from death, returned to heaven, and sent the Spirit to lead us into life, to strengthen us for this life and to bring us joy in this life. We give you glory, adored Trinity, for love so deep, so high, and so broad. Thank you and amen.

289.

Amazing Love, love exceeding all other loves, the delight from above has come to build a home within me. Jesus, source of all mercy, the seat of endless love, come with your saving power to aid my fearful heart. Breathe calmness and steady my racing heart. Lord, I know I sometimes run after death. Train me to pursue you, to seek life. Be my all in all. Set me free. Free to worship you as my true heart desires, praising you always, sharing in your perfect love. You've begun a good work in me. Bring it to completion. Day by day, decision by decision, may I be transformed into the perfection you intend for me so I will be ready to take my place in your eternal presence. Thank you and amen.

290.

Baptism makes me whole by the work of the Spirit and clean by the work of the Son. Daily, I experience these promises fulfilled as Jesus shares his identity with me, and I join with him in his death and resurrection. Amazingly, this sharing brings forgiveness and freedom, marks of the one who is a child of the Father. Faithfully, thankfully, joyfully, I sing your praise Father, Son, and Holy Spirit. Thank you and amen.

291.

Grace and glory are your nature, God. Pour your power upon your people; let us live by your grace and bring you glory in our living. Grant us wisdom and courage to face the challenges of these times. Evil struts, denying the Lord of love; deliver us from the fear that keeps us quiet, holds us captive. Free our hearts to offer praise born of faith. Lord, the world is broken with war. Even your church gets caught in its spell of hate. Pride is the source. Let us who belong to you begin the humble return to your ways of love and service. Begin with me: break my selfishness, let me strive for richness in your kingdom values, not worldly prizes. Thy kingdom come. I will keep my eyes fixed on you, God of our salvation. Such focus will keep me from veering off your path. Populate my day with reminders of your glory, reminders that will hold me to my heart's desire: serving you. Thank you and amen.

292.

The wind is blowing fiercely across the bleak garden outside my window. There are no leaves on the trees. The perennials left are brown and lying flat on the ground. Jesus, were you born into such a winter landscape? Maybe the earth needed to be sleeping and dormant to receive your life and rule. Is this a picture of how to ready myself for your birth? To rid myself of the flash and showy, to let myself be quiet and receptive. I know you were born in a stable, with a manger as your cradle, very elemental. Be born in my simple and unadorned heart. Thank you and amen.

293.

Lord, I admit my heart is dry. I thirst for you. Please, soak me as the morning dew covers the grass and rain fills the ponds. As flowers wilt for lack of water, my heart wilts but does not despair. When will you shower me with the sight of you? It is for you I thirst. Come Holy Spirit. Thank you and amen.

294.

Feel the ache of your Lenten fast. Let your hunger or thirst lead you to the deep place where God awaits. A deer yearns for running streams, wishes winter was past and spring's warmth was here, melting the frozen rivers. My winterish soul yearns for God, longs for the new life and joy spring brings. My thirsty soul, dried up like a raisin, wonders when God will water my being? Tears, my only hydration, have sustained me. They've kept me alive. They've connected me with the idea of you, God. My tears prove I am made for more. They demand satisfaction. I follow them. They take me deep within my soul, where your voice is clear and constant, and I am surprised by your passion and swallowed by your power. Selah. I return to my every day, and your loving-kindness comes toward me. Praising you becomes the song running through my head that will not disappear. Even when I feel forgotten or sorrowful and have reason to complain, I will remind myself to hope in you. Hope in you generates genuine joy. You are still my savior and my God. Lord, break my heart over the reality of my sin. I cry to you from a numb heart. Let me not take for granted your abundant grace given freely. I need your mercy. Oh Spirit, disturb my peace so that I run to Jesus, claiming his cross and his mercy as my cleansing power. God, your mercy loved me when I was too ashamed to even look to you. You saw my anguish and called me home. Through the door of your mercy, I walk into forgiveness and freedom. Thank you and amen. [A prayer based on Psalm 42]

295.

Lord, I could sing of your love forever, for you continually bring me to a new, rescued life. I come to you, and you relieve me of my burdens; I come to you, and you set aside my guilt. Your offered blood puts sin to shame; your quiet submission makes the love of God manifest. Oh if only the world would recognize your amazing love. This daily life of mine drains me. Without your living water, I would run dry. I run to the spring that satisfies. I drink and am renewed. How could I resist your drawing love? How can I show you how much I love you? Thank you and amen.

296.

Settle down, my soul: remember the Lord is with you. You can trust him to redeem all your grief and pain, so bear sorrow patiently. Your Lord will faithfully provide all you need to endure and even flourish. Your friend Jesus will lead you through the maze into a place of joy. Hasn't God been with you in the past? He is as sure today as he was yesterday. So, let your hope remain steady, your confidence unshakeable; what you don't understand today will be made clear in time. The

Galilean storm obeyed his command, and the storm in your heart will heed his word as well. Be calm, my soul; let the one who is familiar with sorrow comfort you in your loneliness. Count him as your best, your truest friend, and look for the companionship he surprises you with along your journey. Take courage, my soul: you are headed for complete union with the Lord who loves you. Disappointment, grief, fear, and sorrow will all vanish; love and joy will be perfected. Oh my soul, live today for that day. Thank you and amen.

297.

Lord, I look to saints who have faithfully gone before me as models for living the Kingdom life. Remembering Joseph, spouse of Mary, I recount his honest and obedient responses to your call on his life. He was faithful to the mysterious trust you asked of him. He cared for Mary and Jesus through uncertain times. May I follow your call and carry with me the ones you've given me to love even when I don't understand why you're leading in such a manner; may my trust in you trump my reason. Thank you and amen.

298.

The more I am aware of your love, the less I am afraid! I have no need for anxious thoughts. I will put on courage as I run the race set before me. The challenge might be taxing, and without your strengthening power, my human spirit would faint. Your help is ever new, ever young and everlasting; your spring of life is ever flowing. Hydrate my soul, grant me resolve, energy, and direction as I make my way toward the finish line. I belong to you. You are trustworthy; I am your beloved. You will keep your promises. Thank you and amen.

299.

God, you are my safe place. You never let me down. In the wash of life, you are my help. The enemy of love wishes me harm. He has great power to influence; apart from you, I couldn't hope to stand against him. You, Lord of all, conqueror of death, strong and unchanging, share your life and victory with me. Fear has no room in my heart, for your truth fills it. Thank you and amen.

300.

Lord, your tender heart desires comfort for the ones you love. You invite me to lay aside my sorrowful load and to walk out of my darkness into your presence. Remind me of the peace that waits for me when I turn to you—peace resulting from forgiven sins and strife abandoned. Oh Lord, thank you that you not only pardon my sins; you blot them out. I've acted in ways that should earn your anger, and yet you see only my broken soul's attempt to be safe. Your realistic love gives me hope. I can be done with my poor patching together of life and receive your spring-like peace and gladness. Your kingdom has come. I prepare my heart to receive you; the valleys of my life rise up, the hills bow down, the crooked is made straight. Come reign in me. Reign over this broken world at last. Thank you and amen.

301.

Jesus, crowds flocked to hear your words and be healed; I come today wanting to hear your voice of love and asking for your power to heal and comfort. The well doesn't need a doctor, the ill do. Come, great physician, touch the wounds of the world with your healing hand. Do not tarry, for the need is great. Begin with me and through me; touch the world with your saving love. Thank you and amen.

302.

Light has penetrated the dark, spreading slowly, pushing back death with its growing gleam. Your advent is my light. and welcome as my morning coffee: longed for, fragrant, dependable, needed. I draw near you, so you can more easily take the burdens from my back and help me take off the heavy coat I wear. I am with you, and I am warm and free—all because you became a child, one who has the power to bear the burdens and coats of the world. I call you what the scripture names you: the one whose rule is peace, the one who is without beginning or end, the wisdom of the universe, the comforter of all souls, the one worthy of adoration. Lord, may your power and influence increase and your justice never end. Begin with me. Thank you and amen.

303.

I breathe in, and my lungs fill with life-giving air. Pause. Breathe. With each breath, I take in your Holy Spirit. Fill me with a new life—one full of love. Send your purifying power to the depths of my heart. Let it beat with desire for union with you. My body carries on by your grace; carry it into eternity. Today, though, may I live as perfect a life as I am able, powered by your holy breath in me. Thank you and amen.

304.

Lord Christ, you are risen, and you woke me early to lead me in resurrection! Thank you. The earth awakes to your growing day, and the heavens declare your beauty. Increase my joy, and I'll hold my victories up to you. Praise you. Lord, your resurrection killed death. It has no power any longer. It cannot block the door to heaven. You live, and death fades away. Ha! I live because you do; today, grant me the grace to follow you into death and resurrection. Then I will have cause for celebration and give you praise and glory, for yours is the victory, and you share it with me. To know you and to live for you is the bliss of eternity. Thank you and amen.

305.

Your love, so deep, so wide, so high, beyond my comprehension and imagination, led you to become a human being for the sake of humankind. For us, you were baptized, fasted in the desert, and faced temptations. For us, you prayed, taught, and worked wonders. You sought us and still seek us. Thank you and amen for so wide, high, and broad a love.

306.

Like Bartimaeus, I cry for mercy. Blind, I hear your voice and feel my way to you. You ask what I want, and my response surprises me. I want to see your beauty in every face I see, to search for your likeness in the actions of the people around me, to tell them how they resemble you, to call out the God-image imprinted within each of them. Maybe they'll begin to believe who they are and act like the God who created them. What a better world this would be. Lord, have mercy. Thank you and amen.

307.

Jesus, you are the solid ground on which I stand, my goal, and my boundary. You are the beloved son and my constant help. I can trust you completely. Knowing your love is consistent and true calls forth a song of praise from my grateful heart. Come, Lord of all, with your usual grace and listen to my heart's plea: to walk in your ways, to have my loved ones know you, to be useful for your purposes, to be a peacemaker in this broken world. I give you my praise, loving God, risen Christ, empowering Spirit. Thank you and amen.

308.

Loving God, hear my cry for help, for I am weighed down by the ways I've fallen short of love. I seek refuge and find hope in you. Gently examine my life and grant me the grace to see the ways I've violated your love's desires. May I have the courage to make right what I can and the resolve to live right today. I count on the prayers of the saints to intercede on my behalf, as I do for them. I seek reconciliation, first with you, then within my varied self, and then with my brothers, sisters, and all creation. Such is the way to peace and joy. Thank you and amen.

309.

You are my God, have mercy on me. Who else can I expect to show me mercy, to know me so well and still be able to offer me love? You, my God. You are good and forgiving, full of love. My pride rises against me, and unkindness seeks to rule my life. They tempt me to ignore you. But you show me mercy and compassion. You wash over my pride and unkindness like a wave over a sandcastle; with every wave of mercy, the castle dissolves. Soon there will be no evidence of its existence at all, except in memory. You do not hold anger over my brokenness. You overflow with love, and your truth is what you share with me. Please keep me in your sights this day. Show me pity. Thank you and amen. [A prayer based on Psalm 86]

310.

Kind Creator, hear my heartfelt prayer, born of a desire to be attentive to your wisdom. You know my weaknesses. Grant me your strengthening grace as I seek your heart. Hear my confession: prideful, forgetful, short-tempered. Hear my testimony: eager, hungry, yours. For your glory and my joy, grant me forgiveness and health. Thank you and amen.

311.

High King of heaven, reclaimer of the world, to you I lift my eyes; I have fallen short of your standard of love. Hear my cry for mercy. Jesus, you sit at the Father's right hand. You are the cornerstone of all creation, the path of deliverance, the door that leads to the Kingdom. I am stained with wrongdoing. Hear my cry for mercy. I trust your mercy, and I admit my need of you. You look at the whole me, the broken and the beautiful, and receive me into your pardon. Thank you and amen.

312.

Lord, many are the saints who lived faithfully and died without renown; with hope and love, they bore their griefs and exalted in their joys. The world's notice they did not have, but yours they did, which was enough for them. Lord, let me be content with your well done and not need the applause of the world. I long for a name that endures, given by your blessing. Lord, let me live in the intimate anonymity of being known by you. Pride be gone, greed be quiet, grace and love increase. Thank you and amen.

313.

As a river refreshes all she touches, open my heart and my hand to freely bless those whose lives I touch. Your mercy found me on the banks of loneliness and brought me home; I am forever yours. Your goodness gave me gifts and graces to share with the world; let me not hoard what is mine by gift. In giving unto others, I am giving unto you. Lord, you love a cheerful giver; increase my joy and my generosity. Thank you and amen.

314.

Constantly giving God, from your riches, you generously provide a wide range of gifts: the beauty of nature, the wisdom of Jesus, his costly cross, the shattered door of death. You've given me so much, and I offer back to you my life and my praise. Thank you, giver of all my days. My skills and time are mine to spend; guide me today in their use. Let me not use them to advance my agenda; rather, I offer my God-given talents to serve your Kingdom. Let me be generous with the resources you've given me. May I be willing to go without so that another can be healed, be fed, or be clothed. May your good news be spread through my life and my gifts. Thank you and amen.

315.

The winter of my life (or my day, or my vocation, or this season of life, take your pick) draws near. I take comfort in knowing I am not alone; you abide with me. Your help is my only sure support. Friends and family love me well, but not perfectly as you do. As I experience the decline in my body and the world, I rely on your unchanging name. No hour passes without my need of your power to guide me away from temptation and toward the light of obedience. Yes, worries have weight, and sadness has tears, but death has no sting; your blessing is my triumph and my goal. Heaven's morning breaks the shadow of night. Lord, you abide with me in sickness and health, in life and death. Thank you and amen.

316.

Oh, Savior, my hope, the desire of my heart, the only source of re-creation, you who created the world are its saving power and its loving authority. You have burst the bonds of death, paid the fee to bring me home, and now sit on the throne of heaven surrounded by and emanating glory. Jesus, be my joy in every moment, my hope of future reward, my only glory beginning (again) now. Thank you and amen.

317.

Mercy marks your character, oh bread of the world, wine of the soul. Your words give life. Your death kills sin. Look on my sorrow, my fear, my waywardness; show me your grace. It is all I count on. Thank you and amen.

318.

Sometimes, I experience perfect peace. At other times, anxiety fills my body and mind. My current emotional state doesn't change my confidence in your intention for my good. When I feel blown down by trials and temptations, I remember that you remember me; you know my frailty and have redeemed me from the storm. You have removed from me the penalty of my sin, and the practice of sin lessens as I gaze at you. Praise you, Jesus. Now I see your face in part; one day, I will see you in whole, and the good you have for me will be mine completely. Thank you and amen.

319.

Oh Lord, oh faithful Jesus, you know each of your lambs; you know what each requires. Give comfort to the mourning and hope to the troubled. Walk next to me, so we can exchange whispers. Bless my work and my efforts at love, and grant me the wisdom to depend on you. Let me sense your presence as I go about this day. Unite my heart with yours so that I want what you want. Then I will know your glory and share your wonder. Thank you and amen.

320.

God, your great love surpasses all human loves. It brings the joy of heaven to my daily life. It makes me at home with simplicity and surprises me with extravagant mercy. Jesus, you are complete compassion, pure and unending love. Your saving power comes to call, making bold my trembling heart. Continue your good work in me, oh Lord. You've begun my re-creation. I'm on my way to purity and wholeness. Grant me eyes to see your work in my life, the way you have changed me from one degree of glory to the next. My eyes of faith see me before you in heaven, offering you the fruit of my life, embracing and embraced by wonder, love, and praise. Thank you and amen.

321.

Lord, Jesus, following you makes my love and my work holy. You promise to show up as I do my work; write a sentence and your presence is given to me. Meet with a seeker, and in her face I see yours. Wash a dish, and I recall your cleaning of my heart. Working with others gives your spirit a chance to bind us together; working alone allows me to commune with you. You are present whenever I enter the marketplace, you long it to be a place of respect and honor. Remembering you in the work and activity of the day makes all of life a sacrament. Thank you and amen.

322.

Oh Lord Jesus this is my hope: to have a spotless heart, to breathe purity, to shine with the light of love; to overflow with joy, to produce the fruit of beauty, to bear your delight. Staying near your cross and not letting sorrow mar my love for you gains me such hope. Fixing my eyes on you, not on myself, gives me the strength to endure the grief that comes my way. Lord, loving you keeps my heart tender, which makes it more easily stabbed. Like your wounds, transform mine into a crown and lead me to your side. Thank you and amen.

323.

Oh, Jesus, your light comes to me as the dawn comes to the earth, tenderly and with ever-increasing brightness. You wake me from sleep's small death, calling me to life. As I sip my coffee, I wake more completely and greet the brightness of the life you've given. My hands relax and receive the gifts and talents you've placed in them. I can trust I am fit for whatever this day holds because your loving hand holds me. At this beginning of the day and with every generous gift of the day, I praise you, Father, Power, and Light. Thank you and amen.

324.

Sometimes it seems as if you are the sun, hidden behind the eastern mountains. I see evidence of your presence in the lightening sky, but I do not feel the warmth of your radiance or the brightness of your face. I long to see you, come, beloved Lord, come before the hope in me faints. My mind often lives in the worlds of "if only" or "tomorrow," false worlds that keep me bound in the chains of sin and borderline despair. I long for the day when I experience completely what I have hints of on this morning, your presence energizing my songs of praise, your glory my one concern, and your love rising within me as the sun always does over the eastern mountains. Thank you and amen.

325.

Settle down, my soul, the Lord is near you. Trust God as you carry the sorrow and the pain your circumstance requires. God cares for your life—every aspect of it. He remains faithful through all the ups and downs, the ins and outs. So settle down. Your best friend, your shepherd Jesus remains near and guides you to a place of rest and blessing. Settle down, my soul, God will prove himself as faithful to the future as he has been in the past. He has promised a bright arrival to your forever home. Don't worry, maintain your hope; even though the winds blow and the waves rise, his voice still rules their patterns. You can trust his care. Thank you and amen.

326.

A forever home awaits me, filled with riches and abundant blessings. It helps to remember this when my heart is low and my song quiets. I imagine the joys in store for me—the bright honor and contented heart that outshine all current blessings. A forever city awaits me, filled with singing, joyful angels, and satisfied saints. The Prince abides within its walls, the weather is as pleasant as a late summer evening, the grass is freshly mown and glistens with dew. I am away from my forever home for a brief time; my sorrow will pass, my worries will end. There will be no tears in my forever home. What a trade-off! A little toil now for eternal peace. My frame of mortality and sin was exchanged for a blessed mansion in the city of the Prince. Hold true, oh heart of mine. The prize is glorious. Choose obedience, my soul, and gain the light; let your hope grasp the glory until hope is no longer necessary because you hold the prize in your hands. Oh fading body, be full of joy, for the Lord is yours completely, and you are his, and only his, beginning now and on into eternity. Thank you and amen.

327.

I am a child of the King of Heaven! I am on a journey. I carry a love song for my Savior as I walk. The lyrics describe his beauty and his wonder, all he has done for me and is doing for me. His glory surrounds me as I walk toward home. My true home is with the Father of Heaven. Many have gone before me on this journey and have arrived at their home with joy, and I am right behind them. I will someday share the complete and perfect happiness that comes with fully entering into the Kingdom. I keep my eyes on the journey. I see glimpses of the light of home, where I will dwell forever with my Lord. Thank you and amen.

328.

Oh Father, creator, and Lord of all, we adore you. The universe proclaims your mystery and your power. You spoke, and planets, stars, and galaxies came to be. You assigned them their place and their course. Perhaps the order of the sky reveals your face. It certainly reveals your glory. In quiet awe, we recognize creation's praise of you, and we add our voices to tell of your wisdom that never ends. Thank you and amen.

329.

Lord, Jesus, your words are life. There is no other source of wisdom and peace that compares. Some hear your voice; I do not. It is by faith, not by sight or sound, that I believe your nearness and care. In the moments when I doubt, Lord, help my unbelief. By faith, I will seek you and call upon you, and one day, I will no longer need faith because I will see you face to face. Thank you and amen.

330.

Consider, oh my soul, before you die and move on to the afterlife if you have a worthy treasure. Think about where you will spend eternity, where you will arrive with joy or with mourning. When youth has faded, when breath is hard, when sight is dark, when you are about to die, how will you survive the pain of body and spirit, unless you know the Redeemer and cling to the cross that saves? As I check my soul, I am grateful that I do know my Redeemer and that I live for eternity. I am on an upward course. I tack, sure, but always moving toward Jesus, my savior. Thank you and amen.

331.

There was a man whose career choice made him wealthy but hated by his countryman. You walked by him, looked into his eyes, and said "Follow me." (Matthew 9:9) He did. He left his job, the comfort of the regular income, and went all-in with you. Lord, I have wealth and possessions. I will hold them as a steward, not an owner. All I have and all I am belongs to you. Grant me the grace to hold loosely the many gifts you've granted. Thank you and amen.

332.

Lord, all you do is founded and created out of your wisdom. I look out my window at the wonder of green, blue, and pink, at the gentle dance of the leaves on the shrubs and the birds foraging for seed. I cannot help but think of your creative and sustaining power. I must pause in awe. The sun rises each morning, shedding light on your wonderful works. The moon is a calendar, marking the passing of time. The stars glitter in honor of you. As tremendous and ancient as these wonders are, you hold them in your hand. All point to your greatness. I must join the chorus. Together we sing of your great work and tender care for all of creation. It begins now and will continue through eternity. Thank you and amen.

333.

Creation is also a metaphor for the vastness of your character. The unending skies tell of your love that continues unabated; full of stars and clouds, the skies describe your constant truth and guide my journey. Your justice, like beautiful Mt. Shasta, rises from the level ground, able to be seen from a distance, seemingly impossible to scale, calling to adventure and shelter. Your judgments, like the ocean deep, are impenetrable, life-sustaining, mysterious. You care for all living creatures, both humans and beasts. Thank you for that. Let me grow in appreciation of just how precious your love is for us all. I can count on you for refuge. I live in your house where rich food abounds; I drink from the stream of your delight over me. You are the beginning of my life; I can see the world because you grant light to my eyes. Let me always live in your love and let your justice be my guard. Glory to you, Father, Son, and Holy Spirit. Thank you and amen. [A prayer based on Psalm 36]

334.

Today, dear God, I can depend upon your strength to be the power that animates me, your might to be the trust that holds me still, and your wisdom to be the goal that guides me. I remember your eyes are ever on me, your ears hear my every utterance, your lips are always speaking into my heart. You are my friend and are always beside me. I declare your way is my way today. You protect me as we walk; you have placed a shield around me that defends me against the enemy's intended harm. I am perfectly safe with you standing near me. Thank you and amen.

335.

Lord, create in me a passion for your word and a hunger for a simple life that seeks you in all my studies and my day. May our life together benefit all who know me. Today, grant me a quiet and persistent approach to you; and may I with confidence declare your truth in word and deed. Open your word to my searching heart, share treasure with me that increases my spiritual wealth. I welcome the silence of our companionship, you have won me with your humility and love. Thank you and amen.

336.

Lord, ten lepers, living in isolation, covered with sores and scars cry out to you for mercy. You cleanse them of their disease and restore them to the community. I bring to you, my compassionate Lord, the wounds and sores that plague and remove me from healthy relationships, in particular: cowardice and selfishness. As you did to the lepers do unto me, cleanse me, grant me fresh hope, make me brave and humble. From this place of wholeness, I offer you a grateful heart. Thank you and amen.

337.

Jesus, you bring the peace of heaven to my life. You show me the glow of the Father. You pour out a fountain of light that never ends, that eliminates the shadow and deep of night. You are the holy sun that shines forth love; let your beams of radiance fall upon me, and let your light reach my innermost secret places with the purity of the Holy Spirit. May all your actions on my behalf result in a deeply rooted faith, a subdued false self, and a converted mind that thinks as you do. Let truth become me, let peace rule me, let joy fill me. From this foundation, my day will pass with gladness. My thoughts will be like the unadulterated sunrise, my love as warming as the noonday sun, and my hope like the palette of color left in the western sunset sky. Thank you and amen.

338.

Ah, how amazing! You, the King of all creation, remain near to me when I call out to you. You bend down to hear my whispers, my hesitant words of need. Your warm, calming response to my stuttering increases my confidence, and my voice grows loud with words of praise and rejoicing because you are my God, my near one, my Savior forever. Thank you and amen.

339.

You build up Jerusalem; you bring back Israel's exiles." (Psalm 147:2) Your business is restoration and reunion. I am your Jerusalem. Your love, my great foundation; your presence the bones of my existence. Brick by brick, plank by plank, your work continues. I am becoming a city worthy of your glory. You make me spacious and welcoming, easy to navigate, with plenty of spots to be surprised by beauty and rest. Build up your city. Reinforce the walls of my life, securing me with a means of protection, boundary, home. Decorate me with splashes of color and whimsy. Let your praise be the roof that rests on me. It keeps me safe and warm. Hold me as your precious city. Build me up. Let me be a refuge to the weary, an adventure for the explorers, a resource for the seeking. Build me up, your Jerusalem. Thank you and amen.

340.

Jesus, my Savior, calls with the voice of love to all who are weary and burdened to come and rest in him. I will heed this invitation and come to him. I will lean on the breast of my loving Savior and find reprieve from the sorrow that wearies me. The world's rest does not restore. It doesn't save me from trouble. It doesn't fulfill its promise of peace. Once I've come to Jesus, and drunk from the fountain of living water, nothing else will satisfy me. Thank you and amen.

341.

Unload all your worries onto Jesus because he is looking after you. Worries about money, worries about security, worries about kids, worries about vocation, worries about health—transfer all these worries from your backpack into Jesus' backpack. I cannot carry these burdens despite my efforts, and even though your back bends with the weight of the cross, Jesus, you ask me to add my worries to your load. Thank you, Jesus, for taking away my worries, for looking after me so perfectly! Because of you, I am forgiven and can live freely. I can stand straight because the burden of my worries is lifted. Thank you and amen.

342.

He is the way, the doer, the suffering lover. I am the lost, the idle, the ignorant loved one. Lord, have mercy and grant me eyes to see your love and love to ease your suffering. Love is what provokes obedience. Let me love you more today than yesterday, more this morning than last night, more this minute than last hour. More love… Thank you and amen.

343.

When you restored me to freedom, what else could I know but joy? Grace became the story of my life, grace received and grace given. Your kindness is beyond my understanding; it seems a dream, too good to be true. And yet, how can I doubt your presence when my dreary and dreadful fears are gone! My tears are exchanged for cheers! Joy flows like a river. I will drink from its stream, I will fish from its bounty, I will swim in its playful currents, and I will gaze at its beauty and wonder. Thank you and amen.

344.

Your mercy is wider than the sea, and you set me afloat upon it. The sea comes to an end, but your mercy does not. It stretches beyond the limits of the vast waters and carries me on its gentle swell. Your justice contains kindness. When establishing right, the elimination of unfairness must be marked by kindness or else it loses sight of the reason righteousness matters. When your justice prevails, freedom reigns. Justice serves your love. Your redemption is without reserve; you held nothing back to bring me home. Bloodshed was not too precious a price to buy my return. And the sorrow you bore translates into joy. Thank you and amen.

345.

There is a path I love to walk on; it is the path that leads to your heart. Show me where this path is, and hold me as I follow it. It leads from right here and now through loving service and obedience to perfection. Let me love to serve you and the ones you love more than I love myself and what I stand to gain. Thank you and amen. [A prayer based on Psalm 119:33-40]

346.

Lord, do unto me as you've done unto saints before me; let your wondrous works of grace flow through me. Your kind love has chosen me; you've given me particular gifts to offer that will bring your loved ones closer to your heart. I give you the glory. May your spirit, invested in me, increase my stake of heavenly riches for the benefit of the ones who you will feed through me. Lord, keep your eyes on me. Grant me grace to follow you into the joy of eternity that begins now. Thank you and amen.

347.

Do not, dear one, fear letting Christ come entirely into your heart. Your heart was made to be his home. He is the means, the boundary, and the goal of your heart. Do not be afraid of the power he brings with him when he rules your heart. He is truth that will not fail; he will enlarge his influence and bless you. Do not be afraid to offer him your complete and utter affection. Treat him as your most favored guest, offer him the best you have, and you will be the one who receives the blessing. When he abides within your heart, he searches it out and reveals its spaciousness. He cleans it and makes it habitable and refreshing, a lovely home with no faults or hidden flaws. With him, you will find rest. Your doubts will be quieted, your longings satisfied. You will find your fulfillment in him, his ways, and his truth. His life will bring you the peace he created for you to enjoy. Do not be afraid. Thank you and amen.

348.

Lord, I don't know the length of my days; that is in your keeping, but I do know that loving and serving you is in mine. While I live, let me obey with joy; when I die, my joy will be complete. Jesus, you walked through the dark door of death into blessed life; I will follow. It is so sweet to know you now; I can't imagine the glory of seeing you face to face! May I remember my end this whole day long and live as if it is my last. Thank you and amen.

349.

May your love abound in me, may I care for all people in my world without distinction between the great and the lowly. In the ways I am rich, teach me the wisdom of trusting you not my resources. In the ways I am poor, grant me patience to believe your good word. Give me eyes to see the child hiding within each person I meet, let me call her to my heart with tenderness and warmth. May I bring aid to my stumbling brothers and sisters and may I enrich the lives of those who know me. Thank you and amen.

350.

You have abundant and generous grace, able to cleanse me from every sin. Your healing flows like a gracious river, making me and keeping me pure from the inside out. You are the fountain of life; I drink deeply from your living water. Rise within me; raise me to live in my eternal stance beginning today. Thank you and amen.

351.

It's all about you, God. All I can do is place myself at your mercy. I give up, worn out by the facade of sin, weary from maintaining the habits of death; I beg you, do not cast me away, create a pure heart within me, and give me a faithful spirit. "I" am defeated. It is a magnificent defeat. I want to know once again the joy that comes with dependence on you, the energy that sustains me as I work with your Spirit, being used to bring wanderers home to your love. Joy shall be my song, the melody is your goodness, the tone of my life will be praise to you. I know I can't earn or achieve your favor, what you long for is a heart that knows its true state: beloved and broken. Oh Lord, restore my foundation, repair my falling walls, rebuild my house, so your beauty can dwell and shine from my life. Thank you and amen. [A prayer based on Psalm 51]

352.

You deserve all the credit for my victories in body and mind. It is you who rescued me, even when I didn't realize your power was at work. Thank you. So many people, including me at times, remain in the pit because we don't remember or sometimes refuse to call on you. And yet you revive us when we do. Thank you and amen. [A prayer based on Psalm 30]

353.

Come, let us return to the Lord with hearts that are humbled and repentant. Our God is gracious and will not banish us in our grief. He is powerful; he sends storms, and he stills waves. He can indeed ruin, but he is also strong to save. It has been night for so long, but dawn will come and bring the light. God is the dawn, God will come, and I will join him, completely glad at long last. Thank you and amen.

354.

Oh Lord, you live forever and are the maker of all creation. The sea, the sky, the sun, and the moon all obey your command. Let me remember your goodness and your judgment. People get what they give away. The proud, arrogant, and selfish will receive condemnation. Help me, Lord, to call on you and not depend upon myself. I am sure you will help me when I call upon you. The Holy Spirit sends grace to cleanse me, inspire me, teach me to want the good and reject the bad, and break the power of sin that inhibits my growth. Lead me by the path that leads to your home. Guard me and keep me safe. Thank you and amen.

355.

Jesus, keep me mindful of your sacrifice, for it is the source of my healing. I kneel before your cross; love and mercy pour over me. Your eternal light shines through your broken body, and darkness dissolves. Today, I walk under the shelter of the cross, hoping and trusting in its power to bring me home. Thank you and amen.

356.

Your breath gave life to the dry bones you had knit together through Ezekiel's prophecy; breathe on me. Bring new life to the dry places of my soul, and energize me with your love so I can act on your behalf. Your purity is the oxygen that cleanses and sustains me; union with your will gives me a purpose and power. I breathe in—hope for today and eternity; I breathe out—rest and peace. Thank you and amen.

357.

This is what I can count on today from the God who loves me: strength to pursue life, might to persist in love, wisdom to guide my steps. Your eyes are on me, your ears attend to me, your lips speak to me. Jesus, my friend, you stay close to me. As I walk with you, your protection surrounds me, your power defends me, I am safe. Holy Spirit, drive from me any residue of death and walk me into greater life. Thank you and amen.

358.

Oh, dear Jesus, I am so blessed to be able to talk with you about anything that weighs on my mind. Perfect friend that you are, you listen to my moaning and complaints. I find that when I am anxious or fretful, it is because I have neglected to bring my concerns to you; when I am tempted to wander off the path of life, it is because I have lost sight of your face. How kind you are! You know the turns on the road that will cause me trouble, and you stand there guarding me against danger, keeping me safe, and gently guiding me back on to the path prepared for me. I come to you, for I am weary and heavy-laden. I exchange my burden for your arms of protection and comfort. Thank you and amen.

359.

A melody continually plays within my heart. It's the backdrop of all my life, the tune that will not leave my head. Your promise to remain with me always, whatever may come my way, is the melody of that song. Sin and death had quieted my voice, but you stirred the strings of my heart and taught me a new song—one of hope, not pain. Feasting on your riches, resting under your protection, gazing at your kind face—these are the instruments that carry my tune. Even when the way is rough and the path is steep, you are with me; your presence keeps me singing. We will climb the path together until the day I join the eternal choir of saints who constantly sing of your goodness. Thank you and amen.

360.

I am held safe in the arms of Jesus. I rest in his gentle embrace; his love is the blanket that warms me. In this close embrace, I can more easily hear him whisper words of comfort, murmurings of hope, assurances of love. In the closely held arms of Jesus, I am safe from the corrosive nature of worry. No real harm can reach me when his arms hold me tight. Sorrow causes me to cling to him. Fear moves me to bury my head in his chest. Jesus, my refuge, my rock, I will remain in your arms. Hold me tight this day. Thank you and amen.

361.

Lord, during this time of uncertainty and discord, send me out as a shepherd to speak hope, for you are near to bear with the wounded, to comfort the frightened. Let me be a force for your kingdom—one who is gentle and spreads peace, who rejects the ease of empty material gain. May your grace work constancy and appropriate urgency into my faith. Keep me mindful of your hidden visage in every face I look upon. Every voice I hear echoes a piece of your heart, every word that is spoken or written is born of hope, either realized or disappointed. Let me treat each as I would treat you. Thank you and amen.

362.

Loving God, in your wisdom and love, you chose me to be among the saints who live and die by your grace. Thank you. May this same wisdom and love energize me to share your name through my writing, words, and deeds. In my living today, let me practice dying, for in losing my life, I find it; in dying to my false self, I find my true and best self, shaped by your Spirit into my unique image of Christ. Grant me the grace to follow where you lead this day, bringing your love with me into every encounter. Thank you and amen.

363.

Darkness was all we knew, yet our souls longed for more. We leaped for joy when the glorious light appeared, recognizing it as our true hope. Now, we who once dwelt in death's surrounding night abide in life's eternal day. My joyous heart gathers to hail the rise of the better sun! A child of hope is born to us, an infant who will rule with justice and mercy. His name declares his intent: the Prince of Peace, a magistrate who will settle our discord with his divine serenity; Wonderful Counselor, a source of wisdom who will abide in our hearts and direct our course. Come, long-expected Jesus, may your power increase, your justice rule, and your peace reign over our world. Thank you and amen.

364.

Oh, Lord, I mumble my prayer. As I do, I picture you opening a door, welcoming me into your home, built upon your constant commitment to me. I stand within the walls of your unshakable love while my inarticulate heart communes with your understanding heart. My heart's desires and my soul's needs are already known by you, yet you cherish the moments their demands drive me into your embrace. "I know what's best, can you trust me?" you ask of me. Soaking up the warmth of your presence and clinging to your assurance that all will be well, I settle down. The voices that accuse me of not being worthy of your favor change their tone. The words remain the same, but they change into a confession that admits the truth. These words come not with judgment, only the recognition of reality: You are holy. I am not. Yet I come into your heart of love and am sent out with the membrane of sin that wraps me round, effaced a little bit more. Soon I will be holy as you are. Until then I will return to my home address: God's faithfulness and righteousness. Thank you and amen. [A prayer based on Psalm 143:1, 2]

365.

The one who tends and feeds me, who guides and guards me is the King of Love. All that enters my life must pass through the gates of his love and submit to his law of love. Disease is transformed into greater dependence on Love's power; pain becomes an instructor in sympathy; setbacks teach me Love's humility, and injustice equips me with Love's commitment to peace. Thank you, Love divine and human for supplying all my needs, refreshing water, nourishing bread. Thank you for making a way to walk through death's valley with assurance and hope. Thank you for the legacy of goodness and mercy that will follow me because I am yours. Thank you and amen.

Suggested prayers for various topics

Anxiety 135, 141, 142, 147, 206, 222, 227, 230, 264, 341

Awe 35, 36, 51, 52, 56, 78, 92, 94, 95, 103, 143, 190, 220, 258, 259, 282, 328, 332, 333

Christ is All 175, 210, 211, 276, 321, 347, 357

Easter 129, 131, 235, 284, 285, 286

Faith 4, 5, 8, 74, 83, 111, 196, 228, 297, 298, 324, 329

Fasting 119, 166

Fellowship 53, 231

Forgiveness 6, 20, 46, 59, 113, 128, 200, 239, 308, 311

Freedom 117, 184

God's Faithfulness 14, 15, 43, 48, 55, 60, 93, 97, 112, 127, 169, 194, 198, 201, 267, 275, 278, 296

God's Grace 10, 25, 45, 85, 91, 168, 207, 208, 236, 350, 353, 354

God's Guidance 185, 238, 314, 345

God's Nearness 18, 29, 34, 39, 40, 49, 62, 79, 186, 197, 205, 221, 279, 338, 360

About the Author

Debby Bellingham was found by the love of God when she was 17 years old, and that love has faithfully kept her since then. Her greatest understanding of herself and her relationship with God is that she is beloved and broken. She says, "I wake up every morning eager to hear God's voice of love and then share it through my writing, words, and life." As an author, a spiritual director, and a spiritual formation retreat facilitator, she loves to create opportunities for individuals and groups to experience a closer connection with God. Her training as a licensed marriage and family therapist equips her to understand better the relationship between the spiritual, relational, and psychological aspects of a person's soul. She has served as a pastor in San Francisco; as a chaplain to pastors in Paris, France; and as a youth outreach missionary with Young Life in California. She has a Bachelor of Arts degree in Interpersonal Communications (Sacramento State University), a Master of Science degree in Counseling (San Francisco State University), and a Doctor of Ministry degree in Christian Spiritual Formation (Graduate Theological Foundation). She's a follower of Jesus Christ, a wife, stepmom, grandmother, and is owned by two dogs and a large garden. She lives in the Hudson River Valley of New York. You can check out her ministry and offerings by visiting her webpage: debbybellingham.com. She blogs regularly at thementoredlife.com. She writes a daily prayer and seasonal devotionals.

Visit her at www.debbybellingham.com.

Made in the USA
Las Vegas, NV
24 November 2022

60235954R00096